P9-DTV-417

PENGUIN

ARKANA

THE DREAMBODY IN RELATIONSHIPS

A key figure in the revolutionary field of dream and body work, and of psychological interventions in psychiatry, Arnold Mindell is the author of *Dreambody*, *Working with the Dreaming Body*, *River's Way*, *City Shadows*, *Working on Yourself Alone*, *The Year I* and, with Amy Mindell, *Riding the Horse Backwards* (all published by Arkana), and *Coma, Key to Awakening*. He is an analyst in private practice, co-founder of the Center for Process Oriented Psychology, Zurich and Portland, and analyst and teacher at these centres. He has been a resident teacher at Esalen Institute, Big Sur, California, and lectures and teaches throughout the world.

ARNOLD MINDELL

———————

THE DREAMBODY IN RELATIONSHIPS

ARKANA

PENGUIN BOOKS

ARKANA

Published by the Penguin Group
Penguin Books Ltd, 27 Wrights Lane, London W8 5TZ, England
Penguin Books USA Inc., 375 Hudson Street, New York, New York 10014, USA
Penguin Books Australia Ltd, Ringwood, Victoria, Australia
Penguin Books Canada Ltd, 10 Alcorn Avenue, Toronto, Ontario, Canada M4V 3B2
Penguin Books (NZ) Ltd, 182–190 Wairau Road, Auckland 10, New Zealand

Penguin Books Ltd, Registered Offices: Harmondsworth, Middlesex, England

First published by Routledge & Kegan Paul 1987
Published by Arkana 1992
3 5 7 9 10 8 6 4 2

Printed in England by Clays Ltd, St Ives plc
Filmset in Palatino

CONTENTS

NOTE TO THE READER

I apologize to the reader for the use of masculine pronouns in this book. I am very well aware of the need for gender-corrected language. My preference in using the pronouns 'he', 'him', and 'his' should in no way be taken as a reflection of sexist tendencies; I choose them for the sake of readability and convenience. As a text aimed to the reader interested in issues of psychology, I frequently speak of an imaginary therapist or client. Therefore, I use masculine pronouns to avoid awkwardness in my constant referrals to therapists and clients.

ACKNOWLEDGMENTS

I am indebted to my intimate relationships, close friends, and to the first adventurous students of my relationship seminars in Tschierv, Switzerland and Seattle, Washington. These people helped me to live and experiment with relationship during the crucial phases of my studies.

I am particularly grateful to Barbara Croci for helping me with the applications presented in the second half of this work and to Joe Goodbread for aiding me in clarifying many aspects of double signal and dreambody theory. I am also greatly indebted to Julie Diamond for her excellent comments, editorial work, and typing of the original manuscript. Amy Kaplan was especially helpful in contributing ideas to the final product. Dawn Menken helped me with the typing, indexing, and critical reading of the final manuscript.

The following friends have also added greatly to the manuscript through their support, critical reading, and personal interaction: Jean Claude Audergon, Gisela Audergon, Kim Burg, Urs Büttikofer, Jan Dworkin, Barbara Hannah, Victoria Hermann, George Mecouch, Nora Mindell, Lara and Robin Mindell, Carl and Pearl Mindell, Max Schüpbach, Debbie Schüpbach, and M.L. von Franz. I would also like to thank Eileen Campbell, editor at Routledge & Kegan Paul, for her constructive support and belief in this work.

The work of C.G. Jung helped me to realize that what people do is meaningful; it is neither right nor wrong. Modern family therapists convinced me of the applicability of my earlier studies in physics. Groups do behave in some respects like single systems. Many tools for working with the coupled nature of communication processes, channels, and signals came from my physics studies. My experience in dream and body work described in the *Dreambody*, aided me in understanding group dream patterns. *Working with the Dreaming Body* challenged me to find out more about the relationship of the individual to the collective. The theoretical foundation for process theory and its connection to alchemy and Taoism can be found in *River's Way*.

Carlos Castaneda's don Juan must be one of the spirits behind this work because I dreamed last night, before completing this manuscript, that it deals with becoming a 'warrior' in the city, to quote one of don Juan's terms. In my dream, *The Dreambody in Relationships* was called the 'Warrior in the World,' for it had to do with leading a 'tight' life, in which one realizes that the 'nagual' or unconscious organizes relationships, and thus, every moment could well be the last. In the dream it was said, 'Therefore, be wide awake and use all of your faculties and courage to realize that the binding element in love and relationships is an ally; namely, the process which is now dreaming us all into action.'

And finally, I am indebted to the Research Society for Process Oriented Psychology and the Jung Institute in Zürich for the opportunity of having lectured on the following material.

Without these relationships, writers, spirits, institutions, and historical background, this work would never have come into being.

Chapter 1
DREAMBODY LANGUAGE

I have written this work hoping to be of service to the layman and professional therapist who is pressed to delve deeply into the mystery of relationships and who wishes to acquire the special tools necessary to transform this mystery into a satisfying and vivifying everyday life. Anyone interested in working deeply on relationships, learning how to process issues, and experiencing the dreaming back-ground which creates them is invited to take part in the development of a process-oriented relationship work.

There are three special characteristics of this work. First, it attempts to weave the tasks of family therapy together with communication theory and the dream and body work developed from individual therapy. This interweaving is important because without dream and body work, family therapy can be a shallow experience for the individual.

Second, this work brings together group focus with the kind of individual attention the client usually receives in individual therapy. For modern family therapy which tends to neglect the individual in favor of the group, this is a necessary step. I understand the commitment of the family therapist to the group, a commitment which sees the individual as an aspect of a larger system. But I feel that family therapy which continues to negate or neglect the manifold depths of the individual will eventually lose its power; the individual will feel only partially understood as part of a family system.

Third, relationship is a channel; it is only part of the

individual, just as he or she is only one channel of expression for a group message. Just as each group has as many types of expressions as it has people, so each person has various modes of perception and expression. One can experience oneself in dreams, internal dialogues, body feelings, movements, world events, synchronicities, and, of course, relationships. Thus, relationship is but one way in which we experience ourselves. To make it the only way would be as naive as saying that the individual is independent of the world in which he lives.

Thus, process-oriented relationship work intertwines the tasks of family therapy with the powerful dream and body experiences of the individual; it sees the individual as a channel for the group and relationships as a channel for the individual. This combination is made possible by a fourth characteristic of the book, its commitment and focus upon the process of relating itself, i.e. conscious and unconscious aspects of relationship. The reason for this focus is that thousands of hours of working experience with relationships have shown me that simple solutions, rules, advice, and even understanding are only temporary and, at times, ineffective. As a matter of fact, I discovered that recommendations and instructions as to how, when, and with whom one 'should' communicate create even more troubles. Believe it or not, I have even seen situations in which trying to withdraw projections, the veritable *sine qua non* of psychology, can be destructive to all concerned.

Thus, I deal with a wide range of relationship issues: the patterns behind falling in love, breaking up, extramarital affairs, sexual anomalies, child care problems, aggression, excessive politeness, etc. In all these situations, the most useful way of working is to focus upon the intended communication, the 'dreaming process' behind relationships. Working with this dreaming process not only makes it possible to appreciate and experience the deep stream behind relationships, but also facilitates working with the conflicts at hand. Let me give an example.

Joan and Rolf come to see me and sit across from one another. They are under a great deal of stress and look totally exhausted. They have been arguing endlessly about breaking up and are now at their wit's end. Rolf pleads that he is trying to behave in a more feeling way, as she has been requesting, and Joan is becoming hoarse while reprimanding him for his overly rational behavior. She complains that he talks too much. At this point I decide to bring in the unintended communication into the relationship, namely, her hoarse voice.

'Follow your hoarse voice and be quieter,' I recommend. Rolf stares at Joan as she becomes silent. He continues to look quietly at her and a tear appears in the corner of her eye. Now some feeling moves him and he is also speechless. After a while, she manages, 'I hate to admit it, but I really love him.' They both just gaze into each other's eyes until the session closes. Rolf said that he had dreamed just after their first meeting that their relationship consisted of sitting quietly side by side and gazing at the ocean.

Joan and Rolf communicated in two ways simultaneously. One way involved arguing about splitting up while the other, a 'dreaming process,' was to gaze quietly together into infinity. Staying together or splitting up are conscious methods of defining their relationship which is unconsciously patterned by their common fascination with the seas. Many psychologists know today that people are capable of communicating simultaneously on several levels at once. What might be new is that the unintended communication, the so-called 'double signals' such as Joan's hoarse voice, connect people to a dreaming process which plays a background, yet decisive, role in binding people together.

Thus it seems that people are capable of communicating simultaneously with two very separate languages without realizing it. Their first language, the intended one, consists of the issues and themes they focus upon, such as Joan and Rolf's argument. This primary communication process is so powerful that it apparently hypnotizes those who listen to it, obliterating their awareness of the unintended, dream-like communication process.

This second process, the unintended or less conscious one, is an enigma; people are rarely aware of it or speak about it. Yet the less people pay attention to the grunts, shrugs, sounds, eyebrow movements, sitting positions, and other forms of this unintended language, the more powerful and disturbing it becomes. It creates somatic problems – Joan had just had a throat operation which contributed to making her hoarse. The secondary signals, the double signals, interrupt the primary communication to such an extent that soon couples do not understand each other any more. Conversations around conflicts rapidly become confusing or, even worse, deteriorate into fighting and name-calling, as partners accuse each other of lying or not remembering what they have said or done. The more partners in a relationship become aware of this dream language, the easier, less painful, or even irrelevant working on the primary issues becomes.

I call this second communication process, 'dreambody language,' because its body signals, sitting positions, vocal tones, actions, and reactions can be observed not only during conversations, but also in the dreams of the participants. Learning about this language is a matter of awareness training. Employing it, however, requires patience, courage, and self-knowledge. To use it by yourself, you have literally to bring another reality into your world.

Dreambody language is truly dream-like. We do not quite notice or understand its signals. Its information appears quickly as incomplete body motions, strange notions, or dreams, as well as in beliefs and myths which we do not even realize we have. Joan, for example, was unaware that she did not tolerate silence well, and Rolf believed that he was a very feeling person! This is why all of us, like Joan and Rolf, often suffer from what appears to be beliefs or myths in collision, dreams trying to impinge upon and enrich the everyday world of relationship conflicts, disturbing the body and waiting to be brought into the light of day.

Process work with an individual and with the relationship of which he is a part almost always reveals that the same dream patterns which organize individual life organize the couple or group as well. I will say more later about this organizing pattern which I call the 'global dreambody.' Suffice it to say now that it is a collective dreambody, a field whose messages unfold in process work, revealing that each individual member of a group is one of its specific and necessary channels.

The global dreambody binds us together; it mysteriously organizes our personal psychology and connects us in unseen ways to the inner world of others, creating and disturbing friendships. Living in such a field requires not only love and generosity but a high degree of awareness, courage, and readiness to be one's self, too. What a great relief it is empirically to substantiate the ancient belief that being your complete self, bringing all your individual parts to awareness as they pop up, is important not only for your personal life but for the life of your community as well.

A great deal still needs to be learned about decoding and processing the global dreambody's messages. Process work focuses upon learning how to do this, on how to observe and use nature as one's ally. This book should be understood as a work in progress, as one attempt to follow couples and groups in a relatively objective way. One goal of this book is to employ dreambody, hologram, and anthropos theories in such a way that they free the psychologist from the tendency to manipulate people with behavioral tricks and clever suggestions pulled intuitively from the therapeutic bag of tricks.

In principle, process work means following the way of nature. Process is that which is already happening not what should be done. Process is that which has already been thought of; it is going on whenever people meet or think of one another. It is the organic method which creates relationships in the first place. If we could train ourselves to be aware of processes, we could work with natural relationship forces and avoid the tendency to short circuit life by applying technical strategies or trying programs as short-term solutions.

Thus, in this work I frequently use the term 'process work' instead of 'family therapy' for two reasons. First, people in the midst of family trouble often resist family therapists because they fear that the therapist will favor the institution of the family over the development of the individual. 'Process work' focuses upon the intended and unintended processes, upon what is happening and trying to happen, not upon who should be present, what should be happening, or what roles should be filled.

My second reason for using 'process work' instead of 'family therapy' is that many human problems cannot be understood within the limiting focus of either individual or group therapy. Human beings seem far too complex for the unnecessary limitation of prescribing therapeutic attention to either an individual or his family. Moreover, people are too interesting to be boxed into a 'therapy paradigm,' which implies that there is always something wrong with them. One goal of psychology might be to develop the ability to follow flexibly relationship processes as their focus wanders between individual and collective situations, between the kids and the adults, dreams and body situations, spontaneous gathering and separation, individual dynamics and parapsychological happenings.

The first half of this book reviews process concepts and adapts information theory to dream and body work. The last half focuses on couples and families, stressing the practical application of theory to case material. The implications of relationship studies for global ecology are discussed in the last two chapters.

A film called 'Introduction to Process-Oriented Psychology' is now finished. This film consists of 3 parts. First, is an interview with Arny Mindell. The second part is a beginning work. The third is an advanced work on dealing with strong emotional issues.

Chapter 2
PERSPECTIVE ON FAMILY STUDIES

TRANSFERENCE

As you may know, Freud made relationships a focal point in psychoanalysis through his theory of transference. According to his theory, transference was a neurotic symptom of the fact that patients projected or 'transferred' problems with their mothers and fathers on to the therapist. In fact, in classical Freudian psychology, the therapist indirectly encourages these relationship problems by remaining unknown and unseen. In this classical setting the therapist sits behind the desk while the client lies on the couch projecting the frustrations and dissatisfactions of his relationships on to the therapist.

COUNTER-TRANSFERENCE

Modern Freudians have studied the phenomena occurring between patient and therapist and developed the theory of counter-transference, that is, the doctor's affective experiences of love and hate transferred on to the patient. It was discovered that the doctor often experienced emotions which the patient unconsciously refused to experience. For example, a doctor who feels guilty about asking for money from his patient may be in the position of acting out the client's own guilt feelings of asking for things. In other words, in the modern Freudian view, the doctor, too, can experience feelings which are not only linked to his own complexes but to those of his patient as well.

JUNG'S ADDITION

Freudian psychoanalysis essentially tries to understand and work with an individual as a separate and distinct unit. Simply stated, the therapist comes into the picture either as a mirror image of the client or as an independent unit responsible for 'working through' emotional issues. Jung followed the individually oriented method of therapy and discovered in addition that not only were unsolved parental images projected in relationships, but that *any* unknown within oneself could, on occasion, be projected in a transference situation. For example, a client might project on to an analyst the experience of the shaman or the figure of the wise old man. In negative transference situations the client could project the negative mother or the cold, intellectual father on to the therapist. These negative projections are difficult to work with in therapy, in part because they always have a bit of truth in them. Thus, when the client maintains that he is right about the analyst, the analyst does him an injustice by insisting that it is 'all a projection.'

In contrast to other schools of psychological thought, Jung recommended that in these complicated situations the therapist leave his persona behind, drop his professional act, and admit, in fact, that what the analysand is saying may be, for better or worse, true. If the client sees the therapist as having a tough, father-like image, and the analyst, in fact, has dreamed of such a figure, then Jung would probably encourage the therapist to bring in this aspect of his personal development.

TRANSFERENCE TROUBLES

Jung's suggestion to bring the therapist directly into the client's process complicates things a great deal. As the therapist enters the scene, projections about his authoritarianism are removed. The therapist is no longer thought of as a god, but is now real! Jung even felt that it could be useful for both patient and doctor to meet outside the analytic setting. You can imagine what a scandal this created in the psychological circles of the 1920s and 1930s! Still today, the debate between therapists continues as to whether or not it is proper to have personal contact with clients. There is no doubt that if a therapist really wants to know the person he is working with, it is best to see him outside the normal analytical setting. Otherwise, the analyst is forced to rely on his imagination to determine what the client is really like as a total person. On the other hand, the analyst may not have the time, energy, or inclination to do this. Luckily, there are no rules about this. Each therapist must find his own course.

The main point is that Jung brought the reality of the therapist into the client's process by pushing back the desk and facing him person to person. Naturally, he did not do this with everyone. Some clients require a therapist who is an inkblot test, while others need a more personal confrontation. Relationship in analysis is thus a process which is steadily changing, from person to person, couple to couple, and moment to moment.

The therapist's reality often recreates the same relationship problems for the patient as those he experiences with others in the world. This can be quite positive because genuine problems can be worked on as they actually happen. But on the other hand, the doctor himself now slips into the client's problems and runs the risk of being infected by them. Working with a field of which you are a part requires special tools and understanding.

Open and naked discussion about the transference is rarely enough. The analyst has to work at untangling the projections and showing the client that some of his ideas about the therapist are aspects of himself as well. Very often, however, such candor between people is insufficient for solving serious difficulties. Analytical understanding is not necessarily needed. Sometimes genuine confrontations and battles are required. I have found from my supervision work with student therapists that very few patients actually go to a therapist in order to understand themselves better. Through the experience I accumulated at training seminars where students are allowed to choose other students to work with, I've discovered that one of the many reasons for choosing a particular therapist is that he or she is weak enough to be overcome! The client might need to use the therapist as a punching bag to increase self-confidence. In other situations, the therapist may be used as a mother who unconditionally supports the client. Only in rare cases does the client need a complete relationship in which the therapist develops together with the client. As we all know, therapists are only people; many can fulfill only the client's rudimentary requirements. Thus, the patient often outgrows the therapist. At this point troubles arise which understanding alone will not settle. There is frequently no other way out than to ask a third therapist to step in and sort through the web of difficulties.

The third person represents a special viewpoint. Here we come upon one of the first conclusions of psychotherapy and perhaps one of the most shocking: a deep and lasting relationship is only possible with a consciousness that is directly involved in and also detached from the relationship. The third person is the symbol of a consciousness which is impersonal as well as personal, Taoistic as well as emotional, distant from, yet engaged in, the relationship. The third person represents the capacity to get beyond the one-to-one situation, to see both people as individuals and simultaneously as a unit which is in the midst of suffering because its two parts are not communicating efficiently.

BEING RIGHT

The need for a third person is inevitable because whenever two or more members of a group fight each usually insists upon being right. The conviction that you are wrong or right has nothing to do with the relationship because you could be unfailingly right, you could prove yourself in the highest court in the land, you could show a jury that you are smarter, more intelligent, and more conscious than your partner, and yet you would still have little or no relationship to your partner. Being right is only for the gods, it's no more than a fixed state. At best, it is a judgment, but it is not and cannot replace the living, ongoing process occurring between people.

WITHDRAWING TO INDIVIDUAL THERAPY

Relationship is a process that involves two or more people, consciousness, bravery, and above all, humility. Now, who has all of these? When in an affect, no one I have ever met has all of these qualities. In such a state, the most instinctive thing to do is to feel hurt, withdraw from the relationship, and focus entirely upon yourself. Withdrawing happens in the ordinary marriage battles when one partner closes the door and refuses to speak to the other for hours, days, weeks, or in the case of some divorces, for ever.

Resignation and withdrawal happen in the theory and practice of psychotherapy. In therapy, the focus is held entirely upon the client, and the client does not usually want to know much about the therapist. In a relationship conflict, the client often feels so fed up with his own entanglements that he insists upon studying only himself. This way he can learn a lot about himself, he can decipher his own complexes, and he can discover the patterns of his conflicts, but he can never really learn about himself in the context of his relationships, nor can he understand the process that occurs when he is with another.

INDIVIDUAL THERAPY AS A NEUROTIC ASPECT OF THE THERAPIST

On his part, the average therapist is usually happy about the client's tendency to withdraw. One reason is that most therapists are neither ready nor willing to enter into relationship with clients in which the therapist is forced to look like an average human being. When in a conflict with the client the therapist often gets frozen in the role of therapist; he must constantly be 'right,' for after all, he is supposed to be the more conscious of the two. This assumption manifests itself in the way he thinks or talks about his analysand in private. For this type of therapist, clients are the ones who are sick and neurotic. In his paradigm he is right, and he will wait for his clients to organically or miraculously change. Without realizing it, the therapist, regardless of his school, slips into one of the greatest pitfalls of relationships: believing he is right.

This belief enters into the therapist's work whenever he

takes sides in a conflict, believing, for example, that *his* client is the member of a couple or family most likely to develop. Whenever he thinks that the member of a couple or family with which he works is better than others, whenever he is seduced into a coalition with one member against another, he does his individual client and the family an injustice. Coalition happens so frequently that it is rarely recognized; it's one of the reasons why individual therapy has so often led to the downfall of the relationship.

The model of individually centered psychotherapy needs extension, fresh air, and re-evaluation. It needs relativization by another model: its shadow, the concept of group, family, and community. The latter alone stresses relationships at the expense of the individual consciousness, and the former alone neglects the process occurring between people. For these reasons, I believe that a good family therapist should be at ease working with individuals, and the best individual therapist is one who has developed heart and perspective by working within a collective milieu. Only this way can the environment be seen within the individual, and the tendency to take sides and lose the viewpoint of the third person can be avoided.

THE TEN COMMANDMENTS

It's easy to imagine how and why psychology has become a set of programs proposing various commandments for relationships. One program works at love difficulties by raising individual awareness but fails to consider the direct communication pattern present when two or more people sit in the analyst's office together. Meditation is another program; it encourages withdrawal and repression of anger and aggression. Another method recommends forbidding infantilism and emotion. Transactional analysis states: Thou shalt not be childlike, no maneuvers, whining, or power, please. Among the new communication therapists, sudden outbursts are forbidden and relationships must have no dark shadow. The encounter method encourages the client to express anything he feels without stopping long enough to think about it. Fritz Perls' Gestalt therapy was based on a paradigm that the individual is the center of the earth. This exaggeration of the individually centered model could be understood, in part, as a mammoth compensation for the tendency of the last twenty thousand years to sacrifice individuality for the benefit of community and survival.

FAILURES OF THE INDIVIDUAL THERAPY PARADIGM

One-sided focus upon an individual may be as disturbing as it is beneficial. In addition to the danger of its one-sidedness, there are some outstanding examples of the paradigm's failure that I've come across in my work. For example, schizophrenic behavior so powerfully disturbs the environment that to consider a schizophrenic as a single unit is almost a regressive application of Newtonian physics to a quantum particle, an application which neglects the particle as a manifestation of the field in which it exists. So-called psychopathic states such as criminality and amoral and antisocial behavior are, by their very definition, states that are directly connected to the field in which they occur. Any attempt to understand this behavior without consideration of its corresponding field would be one-sided.

A more common example of the weakness of the individual model is found in pediatrics. I've seen children's problems disappear after working with the entire family. Already at the beginning of the century Freud recognized the importance of the relationship between child and parent. Jung pointed out that it was often useful to work with the parents of a disturbed child instead of dealing with the child at all. Today, through play techniques and process work, many therapists work directly with children. Nevertheless, the interaction between children's diseases and family situations is still not well understood, with the exception of anorexia and childhood schizophrenia.

Synchronicity is another area in which individual focus has insufficient explanatory power. I have witnessed one woman become ill in the same area of her body in which her sister was being operated on. In fact, the pains arose at the very moment the sister was undergoing operation. My client had no prior knowledge of her sister's condition. Such phenomena cannot be explained through the individual paradigm alone.

ORIENTATION OF THE ANALYST TO THE FAMILY

Psychoanalysts looked to the relationship between parent and child for the cause of the child's neurosis and held the parents responsible for the child's condition. Jung was a forerunner in dropping this causal viewpoint by seeing that many of his patients had fantasies about their youth which were, in fact, not realistic, but archetypal. He frequently worked on children's problems by requesting growth in the surrounding adults. The schools of analytical thought arising from Freud's and Jung's theories deal with the child today as an individual unit and have developed play techniques adapted to the child's psychology. Though these analytical schools have dropped the causal viewpoint, they still do not work directly with the child-parent system or the communication system between the family members.

FAMILY THERAPISTS

A family therapist sees the entire family together as a unit. He does not, in principle, only focus upon the child or parent but rather on the field or communication system which exists between them. The usefulness of this paradigm is that a member of a family learns to get along better within a given family atmosphere. Yet exclusive application of this model frequently results in a lack of insight for the individual. This, in turn, leads to superficial experiences for that person and his consequent tendency to see two types of therapists: the individual analyst and the family therapist. Since family therapists don't normally deal with a person's problems separately, the individual in the midst of change must switch schools of psychological thought.

In spite of this shortcoming, family therapists have brought about a startling and somewhat disturbing revolution in our thinking. We are forced to recognize that what happens to us is not only a product of our personality, but we are, for better or worse, strongly influenced by the group, nation, and world in which we all live. We are and we are *not* the center of the universe. We find that we are part of an organization which may have an intelligence of its own! To some this discovery may be depressing, to others it is relieving. For the planet itself this insight could lead to conclusions which may be a matter of planetary life and death.

BEGINNING AGAIN

This brief review of the historical background challenges us to reformulate some of the basic hypotheses of psychotherapy in order to see the individual and the group together as one organic process. The challenge is to find a method which connects individual body symptoms, dreams, personal development, and the world situation to the immediate environment. A useful goal would be to develop concepts and tools which allow us to follow the process of an individual or group as its focus varies, centering at one moment upon individual psychology while in the next connecting the process to the global situation. We must develop our ability to appreciate both momentary patterns and the deeper structures which create and unfold relationships and organize entire lives.

Chapter 3
WORK WITH LOCAL INFORMATION PROCESSES

There are many ways of viewing the individual and his relationship to the collective. The most common way is to see both the individual and the collective as a collection of parts. Any human unit, however, be it a person or group, can be understood not only as the sum of all the individual parts and their processes but also as the interaction between these parts. For simplicity's sake, we can imagine the human being to be a field of interacting parts.

LOCAL CAUSALITY
Various connecting principles have been used to explain the behavior of people and groups. The most common and widely known one is the principle of local causality. According to this method, everything we say or do is either caused by our own machinery or else by someone else's action, comment, or reaction. Most psychological thinking is based upon this paradigm.

FIELD THEORY
From another viewpoint, the interaction between parts or people is seen as the manifestation of a general pattern involving all. According to this model, neither blame nor responsibility is assigned to any of the members. Instead, the emphasis is placed upon the governing, overall situation. This viewpoint is especially useful when dealing with situations where it is difficult or impossible to determine the

sender and the receiver of a message. The importance of the individual diminishes and he becomes a manifestation of a field whose parts may no longer be distinguishable. In this chapter I am mainly concerned with causal communication processes. In later chapters I discuss field theory, simultaneous patterns, and how the different types of processes and principles are linked.

PROJECTIONS

Individually oriented psychology contains many causal elements. It is based on the principle that certain signals originate from one person and travel to another. The first signaller can or must take full responsibility for his message. The person-centered viewpoint relates the problem of a couple to signals coming from a given individual. For instance, if a man tells me about his wife, as an individually oriented therapist, I'd consider what he says as a fact, but I'd also think that it may be a description of himself as well. If he tells me in a loud tone of voice that he's fed up with his wife's aggression, I can see that he's in an affect. His wife may be difficult, but since he's displaying the same tendencies that he's complaining of in her, I'd assume he must be 'projecting' something on to her.

COMPLEX AND DREAM

Jung would say that this man is in a 'complex,' a feeling-toned perseveration, or a feeling which continues without stopping. If we look into one of his dreams, we could see that his 'wife' complex architects his dreams. His whole dream is in some way about her. Jung might say that this man's anima, the feminine part of him, needs help and understanding.

PROJECTION AND SIGNALS

Let's look at projection from the viewpoint of communication theory. The man in this example resembles a disturbed sender, continually sending out the same message even when the intended receiver claims to have gotten it. Let us assume that I, as the therapist, hear his words, his verbal message, and believe that his wife must be terribly difficult. But since he repeats himself, I soon come to the conclusion that somewhere, somehow, someone has *not* gotten the message.

If I listen carefully, I notice that he sends two simultaneous messages. One is the content of his message, that his wife is nasty. The other is the loudness of his voice, and it disturbs me. I don't know how to deal with this loudness. If he is really unhappy, he would sound sad, but since he is so loud, I assume – correctly or incorrectly – that he, too, is aggressive.

DOUBLE SIGNALS AND PRIMARY AND SECONDARY MESSAGES

His primary message is the one he intends to send us, that is, his wife is a nasty woman. The secondary message, contained in the loud tone of voice, is that he, too, is very angry. When the primary and the secondary messages carry different information, we call it a double signal. Hearing two simultaneous yet differing signals makes it difficult for us to relate to the sender and to receive any one of his messages clearly. Double signals confuse us. We believe the content of this man's message, but we also dislike him because we sense his aggression in his angry voice. The problem is that he does not hear his own tone of voice, he does not perceive the projection of his own loudness and nastiness.

DOUBLE SIGNALS AND DREAMS

Double signals in communication theory are connected to complexes in analytical psychology, and complexes, in turn, are connected to dreams. Thus, dreams and dream figures are actually the ones sending out double signals. The unconscious manifests itself through a projection, complex, dream, relationship problem, and the secondary message as well. The secondary messages are expressed through all the unconscious gestures, movements, noises, tones, and expressions of the body.

Take the example of someone I met at one of my seminars, a person with whom I had difficulty. I asked her if she thought we could work out our problems and she said, 'yes' but simultaneously shook her head, indicating 'no'. I mentioned to her that she was shaking her head and she flatly denied it! She was completely unaware of her double signal; her primary intention was to work out our problems, but her secondary message said 'no.'

When I asked her about a recent dream, she told me that she dreamt of a very strong man who went his own way and would not accommodate anyone else. As far as she was concerned, she said she wanted to accommodate me and work our troubles out, but her secondary message, carried in the double signal, was the unaccommodating dream figure saying 'no.' He wanted more conflict, not harmony. But since she did not feel strong enough to stand up for herself, to go her own way and not work out our difficulties, she tried to accommodate me, sent out secondary non-accommodating messages, and found herself in a relationship conflict. She felt that *I* was being very unaccommodating and opinionated. Since she just dreamed of such a figure, we would have to suspect that she was projecting a piece of herself which she does not yet know on to me! A projection is an affect about someone who is the mirror image of a dream figure. Think about that for a moment! From the communication point of view, the woman thinks others are unaccommodating, not realizing her own double signal; what she double signals are just the things she projects onto me and dreams about.

THE WISDOM OF THE DOUBLE SIGNAL

This leads to the interesting discovery that dream figures have their own ideas and their own intelligence. They may demonstrate this through any kind of psychological work: body work, dreambody work, active imagination, gestalt hot-seating, or psychodrama. They are manifested in body symptoms (a lion can be a roaring headache) and fantasies (such as sexual thoughts). Jung found out a long time ago that dream figures were the center of complexes, and, as splinter psyches, complexes have their own intelligence. The intelligence can be observed when an individual's double signals are amplified in dreambody work. Since dream figures appear in double signals, we can say that every double signal also possesses the intelligence of a particular dream figure. Discovering the intelligence of a double signal is usually quite shocking for the individual involved; it usually implies more than the individual can, at that time, admit. As we have seen, the splinter intelligence behind a double signal carries a message that the individual is not only unaware of but may even disagree with!

GOSSIP'S RELATIONSHIP TO YOUR BODY

The projection of a dream figure is also a projection of a part of your body that you are out of touch with. If you continuously chat with someone about an absent third party, then you can be sure that the third person is present and can be found in your double signals. In our first example, the man's aggressive wife was found in the loudness of his voice, and, in the second example, the unaccommodating 'Arny' could be seen in the woman's shaking of her head, while saying, 'yes.' Thus, you can individuate, that is, become conscious of your unconscious, by studying your dreams, working with your body, working on your double signals with a partner, or by simply listening to your own gossip!

WORKING WITH DOUBLE SIGNALS

Now let's return to double signals. Since double signals belong to the total communication process of human beings, there are going to be very many situations in which the idea of making the unconscious conscious will clarify and improve relationships.

WHERE THEY APPEAR

As therapists interested in working with these unconscious signals, we need to know that double signals frequently appear in rapidly occurring body gestures, sitting positions in a room, the directions people face, vocal tones, giggles, breathing noises, and even in incoherent sentences. We almost always create these signals unintentionally. (Hypnotists are an exception!)

WHEN THEY APPEAR
The second thing we must know is that double signals are frequently the roots of misunderstandings and repetitive conversations. Since they are unintentional, *their messages never complete themselves*. Thus, they appear in communication processes as incomplete words or sentences which confuse everyone. They are like splinter personalities trying to speak.

RESPECT
The important question is how to bring these signals to awareness. Naturally, this depends upon the situation and also upon the therapist's creativity. Working with double signals requires a great deal of respect. It does no good to accuse someone of double signalling. For one thing, people don't like to be accused of double signalling or of having complexes; it makes them mistrustful and defensive. But more importantly, no one deliberately double signals. Like a dream or a body symptom, a double signal is a manifestation of an unconscious part. It's a signal emanating from the very part of our body that we are, in that moment, not in touch with. Just as it would be ludicrous to 'blame' someone for last night's dream, so would it be wrong to accuse someone of sending out a conflicting message.

AMPLIFICATION
One of the best ways of working with double signals is to ask the individual to repeat and to amplify them. I could have asked the man with the loud voice to increase the volume of his voice, to listen to it, and then ask him how it sounds to him, what does he hear? Or, I could have asked the woman shaking her head to do it again and discover what or whom she is saying 'no' to.

FORBIDDING
Another powerful way of amplifying a double signal is, paradoxically, to inhibit it. Inhibiting a double signal amplifies the urge, the impulse behind it and brings its meaning closer to the signaller's awareness. Ask someone

who is yelling to whisper, and then ask him to express what is being inhibited by whispering. Ask someone who is shaking her head 'no' to nod 'yes,' and find out what message she prevents by agreeing. Or, ask a child who is biting his nails to sit nicely with his hands folded in his lap, and ask him what he's holding back by not biting his nails. Amplification and forbidding are two ways to work with double signals; one makes the meaning obvious by increasing its amplitude, and the other increases the impulse to signal by decreasing the manifestation.

MIRRORING
It's also possible to bring the signal to awareness by acting it out or mirroring it in the other person. In this way the individual gets a chance to react to himself. A child I work with has a habit of constantly biting his nails. I decided to bite my nails, too. The child looked at me, stopped biting his nails, and asked me why I was so afraid. That was a strong result! From then on I encouraged the child to speak of his fears every time he began to bite his nails.

Mirroring is a way of amplifying that requires a great deal of observational accuracy on the therapist's part. The therapist must not only repeat the physical gesture but must also sit and sound the same as the client. Older children and adults can be asked directly what they see and feel when they are being mirrored.

TAKING OVER
Still another method of working with double signals is by physically intervening with the message. Someone sits on my couch, her head in her hand, and tells me she wished her husband would support her more. If I take over the supporting position of her hand, she becomes conscious of how she is supporting her own head. At this point, she 'gets the message' and can begin to learn how to support herself.

ON INTERPRETATION
It is important not to assume that you know what double signals mean. The messages of these signals are always

changing and uncertain. Signals act like a blackboard upon which we project our own complexes. For example, I really should have asked the man and the woman mentioned earlier what the voice and shaking head meant. Misunderstanding arises because people are unaware of their double signals and also because receivers assume they understand the content of the message and frequently misunderstand it. We project our own psychology on to the vagueness of the double signal as if it were an inkblot test. Thus, the lack of awareness of the sender, coupled with that of the receiver, leads to endless conversations in which neither person has the slightest idea what is being discussed. In such conversations, reference is frequently made to things outside the awareness of both. It's important to recognize the incongruence and uncertainty of double signals and not to assume that you know their meaning; one should very humbly amplify them and give them a fair chance to express themselves.

USING FALSE INTERPRETATION
Because it's possible to misinterpret double signals, it's also possible to use misinterpretation as a method of working with them. The therapist can find out the meaning of behavior by misinterpreting it. If someone is giggling, he might ask, 'Are you happy?' The surprising response might be, 'No, I am really angry, but I'm shy to admit it.' Misinterpreting is especially useful with people who are verbally oriented or afraid of body phenomena. For example, the therapist can experiment with an old man who is leaning back by saying, 'Your leaning back tells me that you are tired and want to sleep.' The man could answer, 'No, you are not very observant. Actually, I would like to leave!'

TESTING
Testing is a method that depends on the therapist's power of observation. It is done either physically or verbally. The therapist tests what he sees or hears by finding out if it is really intended. For example, if a client comes to see me for the first time and casually remarks that 'many people don't

like coming to see a psychologist,' I might test that by asking, 'Do you mean that you do not like coming?' Often the past-tense is a double signal. When someone says, 'Last week I did not want to come,' the meaning of this expands when I notice that my client is sitting next to the door as he speaks. One possible response would be to ask, 'Do you mean that you don't want to be here now?' Two people may come to see me for help, but as soon as they sit down they begin to talk furiously with each other. I can test the information 'we want your help' by slowly moving away or even leaving the room. If they don't notice me, then I'm sure that they haven't trusted their own inclination to work things out and needed my support in doing so.

ADMITTING
Another method of dealing with double signals is to work with the effects they produce: the accusations. The accused is always at least a little, tiny bit, guilty of something. In process work, the accusation and guilt scene frequently resembles the following:

She: Every time he comes home, he never takes the time to speak to me.
He: That's not true. Naturally, I am a little tired, but I always speak to her right away.

As they speak she's facing him, but his entire body is facing me while he speaks to her. I could amplify, forbid, test, or intervene into his sitting position, but working with the accusation is often the easiest method. So I recommend to him, 'Why not admit that what she is saying is true, not only possibly true then, when you come home, but true now, too. Right now you are facing me, and not taking the time to talk to her!'

   He stops for a moment, startled, but then admits, 'Well . . . well . . . , O.K. It *is* true. She dragged me here, I didn't want to come and I hate taking the time to talk about this. I'd prefer to do something else.' She was right after all. Accusations usually concern the past because the accuser is aware only that they happened in the past and does not observe that they are still irritating because they are happening in the present in the form of double signals. The interesting thing about an accusation is that even if it was not true in the past and is not true now, it tends to become true in the present because aggressive accusations create what they accuse. For example, 'You have never loved me!' said angrily will create a loveless situation. Hence, a lot of time can be saved by seeing how and where the accusation is true, now in the moment and then admitting it. For example, one can admit, 'True, I do not love you now because you seem angry, not sad.' Accusations are usually denied because they deal with double signals such as anger, the very information which the accuser is unconscious of. It's blocked from awareness by an 'edge.' (See page 147 ff.) Where the edge is great, I do not push. I only gently suggest that it might be true by pointing out where it is happening in the moment.

ACTING

Playful acting may be used as a method for bringing double signals associated with painful issues to consciousness. I remember working with a couple who had a violent argument the night before the session. At one point in the conversation he turned to me and said with a pout on his face, 'And do you know what I did when she yelled at me? I got so angry and fed up with her that I just got up, walked out of the room, and slammed the door!'

I said, 'You mean you were hurt and upset and left?' 'No, I was simply angry,' he repeated firmly. I realized that I was not doing well in emphasizing his pouting so I decided to act it out. I tested him by saying, 'I think this is what I am seeing in you, take a look and tell me if it is true or not.' Then I got up and acted; I exaggerated what I saw on his face. I behaved like a pouting and hurt child, moving to the door and over-emphasizing his pout. I turned my head to one side, put my nose in the air, pulled my lips down at the corners of my mouth, and said, 'I'm hurt, but I don't want to show it. Instead I intend to walk out and stop communicating, then I hope you'll be upset and guilty enough to come after me. That's what I really want, for you to be guilty, but won't admit it. Even though I don't want to admit it, I want to hurt you and I love you and need you, too. In fact, you're the most important thing in the world to me. So there.'

That worked perfectly. He burst out roaring with laughter, cried embarrassedly, and said it was all true. He took heart, gathered up his courage, and told her straight out, 'I really need you, I love you, and hate to fight. I wish you would be nice to me. I need you to rescue me from my isolation and resignation. Please, Help!' In this story acting out was just the thing they needed. It helped him go through his hurt and brought her to the point of opening up her heart and admitting, in spite of her pride, how much she loved him.

DOUBLE SIGNALS AND STORIES OF THE PAST

There are certain times and certain people for whom working on the unconscious as it manifests itself in the 'now' is incorrect. These people do not want to focus on their double signals; they are interested only in what they are saying. They become furious if the therapist points out that something is happening outside their awareness. They either need to focus directly upon you as their partner or therapist or they need to tell you stories from their past.

It is important to realize that the client knows more about his process than you, the therapist, and that you must be careful not to make a routine out of bringing up unconscious contents, or even of working directly with double signals. Moreover, regardless of what the client focuses on, there is always a message in that focus. For example, many people, particularly old people, will tell you the same story over and over again because they do not realize how true this story is for them still today. Another reason is that they are missing their own reactions to it, reactions which inevitably turn up in their double signals.

Stories can be a method for working on double signals, and inversely, working on double signals can be a way of working on the past. Let me give an example. A man recently came to see me and said he had been suffering from a depression. He also claimed in the same breath that nothing was wrong, he just did not want to be depressed.

He resisted all my attempts to delve into his depression and refused to work on his low, slow tone of voice. So I asked him to tell me about himself. He mentioned that he had been working 'brutally' lately, and that he had been thinking about his grandfather. I asked him to say more about the grandfather. He told me with an embarrassed giggle that his grandfather used to beat him until he warned the old man that if he continued, he, my client, would cut off his own arm.

'Grandfather was just nasty,' he said. But I detected a hole. I asked him to tell me what feeling he had cut off when speaking about his grandfather and he said, 'Well . . . nothing much.' I then acted out the sadness which I heard in his slow and depressed voice and asked him if this sadness which I acted out was true for him. He hemmed and hawed and finally broke down and cried, telling me many painful stories from his childhood.

After he had cried, he felt a lot better. It was the first time in months he wasn't depressed. His process illuminates the rule that if you resist feeling unhappy, the unhappiness takes over altogether in the form of depression, a mixture of unhappiness and anger towards the object causing unhappiness.

I tell this story to illustrate that my client's signals of depression could not be worked on directly without those stories being told first. He needed to drop out of the present and not work on his double signals. He first had to go back into the past, to his family of origin, to fairy tale land. The pattern for his depression was stored in his memories, completely intact and undisturbed by his present situation. The past is real for the client; that is important. Some of these 'past' events are so dreadful that they've been split off. They were too much for the conscious mind and became mythical characteristics of the client. Past memories are always present in the body because the double signals, chronic body postures, tics, symptoms, and gestures represent the reactions which the individual did not have in the past and does not have now in his present behavior. In our case, the man did not consciously react with sadness to the brutality of his grandfather or to his own 'brutal way of working.'

There are many other ways of working with double signals. In this text other methods of accessing unconscious material will be discussed at the appropriate time. It is important to find that particular, creative way of dealing with the unconscious to which the individual warmly responds. As a general rule, body-oriented clients will respond well to physically amplifying and inhibiting double body signals. Verbally oriented clients are more likely to feel at home, to begin with at least, with verbal accessing techniques such as interpretive guesses about the meaning of non-verbal signals.

Chapter 4
COMMUNICATION STRUCTURES

In previous chapters I have been bringing together dreambody theory, communication theory, and depth psychology. Signals, double signals, primary and secondary processes, dream figures, splinter psyches, projection, and gossip are terms which describe the structure of human communication. Knowing communication structures helps the therapist (and client) appreciate the client's behavior. Whenever anyone asks me what to do, I either say I do not know or I tell them to do what they are already doing, but to do it more consciously! Prescribing behavior which is not present is ineffective, unnecessary, and possibly dangerous.*

DEPTH PSYCHOLOGY AND SIGNAL THEORY
Before launching into a discussion of communication structures, it will be useful to trace briefly Freud and Jung's contributions to what is today called signal theory. I have already discussed their work briefly in the second chapter of this work in relationship to transference phenomena. Here I want to investigate the details of their discoveries as they apply to double signals.

FREUD
Freud's study of the affects appearing in transference showed him that his patients signalled 'subconscious' dream

---

* Prescribing behavior doesn't work if there is no pattern for it in dreams or body activity.

material, which meant, essentially, repressed information. He noted that the child-like signals in his patients were unconscious requests to the analyst to be motherly and fatherly. Freud worked with these signals indirectly by analyzing the overall behavior of his clients and by suggesting to them that they may be repressing infantile behavior. Neo-Freudians continue Freud's analytical methods and in addition encourage their analysands to 'work through,' that is experience and verbalize these child-like impulses in the 'transference situation.' Since I cannot do justice to all the approaches here, I would like to refer the reader to the work of Kohut and Miller at this point.

JUNG

Jung's study of the unconscious indicated that any unconscious figure which turned up in a dream could disturb relationships as long as the figure remained unconscious. Jung identified many figures but spoke primarily of the animus and anima in the psychology of women and men respectively. The animus, I believe Jung would say if he were to have used communication concepts, usually appears in a woman's 'double signals' when she sends out an opinionated manner while identifying only with her primary process, let's say a lovely and accommodating personality. 'How nice to see you,' a woman might say while the 'animus' appears in her stiff body. The anima appears in men's behavior most frequently in moodiness. 'I'm not upset,' he might say, while the anima raises his voice to an hysterical pitch.

A man who has been insulted won't admit it, but becomes moody, gets up, and walks out while claiming to be very cool and rational. Jungians would say that he is 'in the anima.' Whereas the animus appears as a male figure in the dreams of a woman, the anima appears as a female in men's dreams.

Jung also spoke of the shadow, a dream figure of the same sex as the dreamer. Jung did not identify the shadow as a communication signal, though naturally the double signals of an unconscious shadow figure can complicate communication. We need only think of the flirtatious female and male figures of our dreams which unconsciously influence our behavior in order to imagine how these figures disturb communication!

Jung worked on dream figures through a combination of analytical interpretation, direct confrontation with the client's unconscious behavior, and 'active imagination' where the client could work alone at home on the dream figures by allowing them to unfold their messages to the ego through written dialogue. In this procedure the dreamer fantasized and played with dream figures, giving them a chance to express themselves in detail, usually through writing.

The value of such analytical work can scarcely be overemphasized because through such imagination, interpretation, and understanding the individual dreamer gets a chance to meet, integrate, and dissolve parts of himself which have been dissociated from the ego and sending out unintelligible double signals. One conclusion we can draw from this is that if people do not understand you, you may consider the possibility that one of your dream figures is sending out unintelligible information because you do not recognize and appreciate it enough.

One of the implicit goals behind individual analysis was to reduce communication difficulties. The fact that it does not always produce such effects indicates that there may be other factors disturbing communication besides an individual's unconsciousness of specific dream figures. Experience shows that even an individual who is very aware of his behavior produces double signals when the figures behind these signals have not appeared in the sender's dreams!

Thus, *communication trouble is not only a function of individual unconsciousness. Trouble can arise in relationships because partners are not aware of how their own signals can be temporarily produced by the double signals of others.*

CONSCIOUS AND UNCONSCIOUS, PRIMARY AND SECONDARY
The term 'conscious' and 'unconscious' have proven useful in individual work, but need refining when applied to the

behavior of groups. Consider a typical example of the couple arguing about the garbage. She is screaming, 'Take it out!' and he groans, 'No!' with an insulted and offended expression on his face. We could say from the individual viewpoint that if she dreamed about an irate man and if he dreamed about a moody woman, she was in the animus and he in the anima.

Her screaming and his moodiness are double signals which require greater awareness. She could work alone with her anger and learn to bring it into their conversations in a useful way, and he could investigate his moodiness and learn to express his hurt feelings in a more complete fashion. Let us call the signals they intended to send their 'primary process.' The primary process communicates the information about taking the garbage out. Though intended signals are closer to awareness than the secondary material and are easier for the communicators to notice, they are not conscious. Thus, I am going to use primary where the term consciousness used to be employed.

The reason primary processes are unconscious is that though our couple know they are talking about the garbage, they can neither stop their discussion about it nor control it. They are only vaguely aware of the myths and beliefs that govern their intended signals. Who takes out the garbage is a complicated issue with roots extending through their childhood, culture, and religion. Usually a little probing is needed to find out which childhood, culture, and religious systems shape the beliefs behind the argument over the garbage.

The unintended information, the background battle between her anger and his moodiness, I call their secondary process. Secondary material is more difficult to reach. The man and woman might admit that they are talking about the garbage, yet they will be unable (in the beginning of their discussion) to admit to the rage or moodiness in the background. Once acknowledged, they won't be able to process these signals easily without training. Thus in process work, the term consciousness refers to awareness, while unconsciousness usually means lack of awareness of primary and secondary processes.

THE ICEBERG ANALOGY

Let me give an example. A woman tells me that she is jealous of another woman and a quick smile flickers across her face. Her smile seems to say something but I do not understand its message. I think it might be a double signal, so I ask her to do it again. I say, 'I am interested in your smile. It is a winning smile, I need to know more about it.' She is a little embarrassed but does it again. This time she says she is smiling because she is embarrassed. She feels she should NOT be jealous. I encourage her to amplify the smile and embarrassment. She says, 'It is as if my father were punishing me by making me feel embarrassed of my jealousy. He says it is infantile to be jealous.'

We discuss the father-daughter problem and she realizes that she constantly makes herself feel guilty for ordinary human needs and emotions such as jealousy. Her primary process was 'I am jealous,' and her secondary one was 'I am stupid for being emotional.' Both were outside her control.

The point of the story is that behind the little smile was an iceberg. There are dreams behind the double signal, too. She dreamed that her father was trying to kill her mother. He had always considered his wife to be far too hysterical. In this woman's process the father, an inner figure, had to change to allow the mother's feelings out. All this was found behind her smile!

MYTHS IN COLLISION

This woman's process was not simply her identified problem, jealousy of another woman. Her process was more intricate than that. She had a secondary process which was against having affects of any kind, and this process was symbolized in her dream by her father and appeared in everyday life by the double signal of her quick smile. This secondary process lay at first outside the realm of her awareness; it was utterly unintended and represented a story or myth which was in collision with her primary one, her jealousy of another woman. We are all stages for colliding mythical processes!

DREAMING UP

Now let us focus on a pattern which frequently occurs in communication: dreaming up. Projection and dreaming up describe two possible relationships one's double signals can have to the signals of another. Think for a moment of the woman above who said 'Yes' to me while shaking her head 'No.' Her primary process was 'Yes, I am an accommodating person;' her secondary one was 'No, . . . ' Since she identified only with her primary one, she smiled nicely but her negative head shake made her unconvincing to me. This head shake disturbed me unconsciously. In fact, I did not even know I was disturbed by her at first, even less did I know what could have disturbed me. Thus unconsciously I began to stiffen and get irritated.

This stiffening response was 'dreamed up,' so to speak, by her head shake, by a double signal. Her negative headshake aroused an unconscious double signal response from me, and we began to double signal to one another. This continued until we were both irritated with each other. Most couples continue this irritation even further, denying that they are even irritated in the first place! We would have to say, knowing her dream of the unaccommodating man, that she dreamed me up and indirectly created an affect in me. After a while she had reason enough to project the unaccommodating dream figure on to me.

HYPNOTIC EFFECTS IN RELATIONSHIP

The reason why we become dreamed up and double signal back is that we are unconscious of double signals. Empirically speaking, most people become so fascinated by the primary processes of a person, that we, as a general rule, pay attention only to the intended verbal statements. As a result, we are blind to their unintended double signals and appear hypnotized. We focus only on intended messages and, as if we were in a trance, we filter out the unintended ones. But this hypnotic trance never fully succeeds. Though we intend to focus only upon what people say, we also perceive everything else that they do. But these perceptions happen unconsciously; we do not know that we are aware of them.

Hence, as in my case, I was unaware of her head shake, and I was also unaware of why I reacted irritatedly to her. Hence, my irritation becomes unintentional and is split off from my intention to be cool. Thus, it double signals back to her. We develop two systems of communication, one of which is intentional or primary, my coolness and her accommodating quality, and an unintentional mode which is dreamed up, consisting of signals reacting back and forth without either of us being aware of it.

Dreaming up was a secondary communication process for us in the beginning of our conversation. It was unconscious and unintentional. Projection (of the accommodating figure) is a primary process; she could identify with her affect against me, and yet its roots are unconscious. Dreaming up and projection help us to understand some of the mechanics of couple's communication systems, and to comprehend where some of the individual responsibility may lie in communication trouble.

In a situation where I do not dream of an unaccommo-dating man, my reactions to her are not projections of mine, but responses evoked by her dream and double signals. My momentary responses are due to the nature of our relation-ship. Each relationship in fact can bring to light special aspects of people which do not necessarily appear elsewhere.

If, however, I dream of such a figure, then I, too, would have to look not only at my relationship to her but at this dream figure in myself whether or not she is present. In a situation where we both dream of the same or similar figures, then my client and I are in for a lot of trouble or fun – as the case may be – in untangling and experiencing our communication processes. We are in what I call a 'noodle soup;' we are both part of the same dish and are going to have to learn to eat it or else find the cook who made the soup in the first place!

In general, the problems bothering couples and groups seem to be a combination of dreaming up and projection. Therefore, working on relationship problems involves not only understanding and experiencing the part of you projected on your partner, but also learning how to get along with the real partner. This requires training in understanding dreambody language as it happens in the relationship itself. For this reason I recommend to the individuals I work with to come with their partners every now and then. It is necessary to develop a consciousness of double signals in order to have a good, working relationship. You must know both your dreams and your body to survive a relationship. Since we are always dreaming, we are always dreaming others up to be parts of ourselves. And because we are constantly being confronted with new and unknown parts of ourselves, we will constantly double signal the presence of a dream figure: be it in the form of a symptom, relationship conflict, or synchronicity. Thus, a good relationship doesn't mean harmony and peace, but requires awareness, flexibility, and an appreciation of the dreaming process.

THE BOUNDARIES OF THE INDIVIDUAL

Dreaming up and projection separate individuals and their processes according to their dreams and double signals. Yet, they cannot be separated as far as guilt is concerned. We cannot establish who dreamed whom up first. At any given moment, both people are simultaneously projecting and dreaming the other up. This is where the boundaries of the individual lie. We have arrived at the border, the edge of the individually oriented paradigm. At this point, we either give up and leave relationships to God, or we break through our own limitations and consider the couple as a single unit. If we do this, we can continue to apply the same thinking we have used until now, but apply it to the couple as if it were one unit.

COUPLE-CENTERED WORK

When we work with two people we are working with six processes: the primary and secondary processes of each and the primary and secondary processes of the relationship. Process work deals with the process in the foreground, the one which is coming up. Hence, working on a couple may mean at one moment focusing only upon an individual, while at another it means focusing on the primary and secondary processes of the couple.

To work only with one of these three pairs without considering the other two is to work with only one part of a relationship. That is a dangerous business for the couple; if we focus on one part of a relationship and ignore the rest, the relationship would be severely stressed.

EXPERIENCING THE DREAM FIELD

Just as it is important for an individual to understand and experience the dream dreaming his body into existence, it is also important for a couple stuck in their primary issues to experience their secondary process, the field dreaming their relationship into life. The easiest way to discover this dream is to watch for the double signals each individual makes and then to encourage them to act on these signals, unfolding their messages. In this way, the dreaming process behind the double signals unravels its story. As the reader can imagine, such work adds a sense of humor to the seriousness of the relationship.

AN EXAMPLE

Consider Bob and Gayle. As they begin talking about their relationship, Bob constantly adjusts his glasses. Gayle listens to him and turns away slightly. She says that she would like him to pay more attention to her. He tells her that he is very busy. Thus their primary process resembles that of many couples. She says she wants more time and attention from him and he says that he is too busy. Their secondary process as a couple is described in part by the way he moves his glasses and the way in which she is sitting.

I focused upon their secondary process and recommended that he exaggerate his double signals; fiddling with his glasses. I recommended that she do the same and turn away. He began to fiddle with his glasses and also put his hands around his eyes. After a moment he laughed because he said his fingers were like goggles encircling his eyes. He wanted to look, examine, investigate, and peer at every inch of her. After amplifying her sitting position and turning away, she said she did not have time to deal with him, but wanted to do her own thing.

How surprised they both were to hear and see the opposite form of behavior coming from their double signals. Instead of more, she wanted less attention, and instead of not wanting to be bothered, he was fascinated by her. They burst out laughing as they acted out the dreambody which organized their relationship. He said that he normally would never think of bothering her. Even at night when he wanted to have sex with her he withheld out of fear of invading her territory. She, in turn, said she would ordinarily never dare to turn away from him because she feared he would be so hurt he would never talk to her again. So here, the couple's dream was the exact opposite of their normal behavior.

Discovering the edges, double signals, dreams, and myths is a step toward discovering the structure of communication and creating a tool kit to give people the richest, most continuous, and fluid relationships imaginable.

Chapter 5
CHANNELS AND SIGNALS

Following double signals is difficult work in the beginning. The therapist must have sensory grounded awareness and knowledge of them in order to avoid being mesmerized by the content of speech, or primary process. Below are some of the typical, frequently encountered signals.

AUDITORY SIGNALS
Auditory signals are considered well-known. The dreamer signals when he comes to a complex word by sending out incomprehensible messages. He uses strange verbal structures, foreign words, or evasive ways of expressing an event or relationship. He raises or lowers his voice, giggles, slows down, or speaks quickly. He stutters, makes mistakes, or inserts the wrong word in the sentence. He leaves sentences unfinished. His voice is of a different pitch than usual. His tone is monotonous or placating, heightened or whining. His breath is erratic or he coughs at certain points. All of these signals are informative and should be checked out to see if they are congruent with the content of the speech or if they are messages from a particular dream figure. If you do not understand someone, the missing information may be in their voice.

VISUAL SIGNALS
Visual output is also obvious but harder to distinguish. Look at the face. Is it pale, heavily made-up, sunburned, puffy? Does it communicate what's being said? Does the dreamer

describe a happy event with sad eyes and downturned mouth? Do the eyes sparkle, are they bloodshot, tired? Do the eyebrows twitch or frown? Are the lips puckered, being bitten or chewed on? Does the mouth smile, twitch, or grimace? All these facial expressions are signals, some of which make me uneasy and others which fascinate me. Sometimes it seems that eyes are inviting us to come closer, but the words tell us to stay away. Look at the head and the body. Is the neck stiff, does the head hang down, is it tilted to one side, turned away? Is the chest cavity caved in, are the shoulders drooping or held high? Is the back straight or curved? Are the hips flexible or stationary? Is the pelvis tilted? Are the legs straight, bent, or crossed? Are the feet tapping?

The way a person is dressed can indicate a great deal about him. Is the shirt open or closed? Is the clothing clean or dirty? Believe it or not, clothing is usually chosen unconsciously. Do not assume that the client identifies with what he or she is wearing. A person's dream figure is frequently responsible for what he or she wears, and you can insult someone if you identify him or her with those inner figures! I'll never forget a parson's wife I worked with once. She had on a very daring dress and I thought she looked extremely sexy. I was shocked, however, to discover that she had not the slightest idea, consciously at least, that she looked provocative. In fact, she became terribly insulted when I put my hand on her shoulder as she left my office. The interesting thing was that she had just worked on a dream in which a night-club singer appeared. She saw this figure when she had fantasies about men, but had an edge, a barrier against being this singer. She did not realize that her shadow, the night-club singer, had dressed her that day. That was the very last time I ever identified anyone with their clothing!

KINESTHESIA

Most kinesthesia is organized by unconscious figures. Motion which is far from awareness repeats itself constantly, but never seems to be completed. It is similar to a twitch or a tic. My son Robin is a good example. He recently came home from school complaining of an earache. While telling me about it, he kept putting his head down on the table and raising it up again. After a while, I recommended that he hold his head down on the table. He got upset and said he couldn't do that. The problem was that he had an edge against being tired. A boy with an energetic nature identifies with his energetic nature, not with the fatigue he has after having the grippe. Therefore he splits off his fatigue which manifests itself in a double signal, in this case, the perpetual motion of putting his head down on the table. He believes he has an earache because it's a symptom which does not necessarily mean that he has to go to bed early! So what do I do? I left him with his identity. I gave him a sugar pill and told him it helps earaches but has the side effect of making one very sleepy. He took it, went to bed for thirteen hours, got up, and went out to play, 'healed.' In this case, I was lucky that the pill put the primary and secondary processes together.

PROPRIOCEPTIVE DOUBLE SIGNALS

Another set of signals is communicated through proprioception, or inner body sensation. Proprioceptive double signals are among the most unconscious. Some people, for example, will shake your hand so hard that they hurt it, others give weak, limp handshakes. Further from awareness is the temperature of a person's hand. I remember a woman I worked with who was a warm, friendly person. But when I shook her hand to say goodbye, she was freezing cold. Her temperature signals were saying that she shouldn't be so warm; much of her energy and warmth wanted to remain within her, for her.

One very effective method of using your proprioception as a receiver is to close your eyes, stop talking, and put your hands on someone. Touch his hands, shoulders, or back. I once worked with a man who constantly looked down and turned his head while we talked. I told him that I thought he intended to talk to me, but really wanted to be silent and look away. I suggested that we just hold hands. I closed my eyes and put my hand on his shoulder and was surprised to feel how fat he was. I told him he felt much softer than he either acted or talked. This triggered a deep, emotional response in him, and he told me a long story about his father who was so cold and tough that, as a boy, my client never felt able to show his father how much he needed soft, feeling contact.

Another crucial area of proprioceptive communication is body contact, especially between partners. Here we come to a social edge because most physical contact in our society is either hitting to express anger or making love to express love and attraction. Just holding and touching without explicit sexual goals is relatively unknown. The desire to make proprioceptive contact with a partner is automatically interpreted as the desire to make love. Not knowing that he wants to make proprioceptive contact, the person usually says that he wants to make love, but emits double signals with body temperature or body fluids. His partner picks this up and gets turned off immediately. If the first person could be congruent with his proprioception and body experience which isn't sexual, there could be contact without the necessary verbal instruction to have sex.

I'll never forget one of the first students I had some years ago. He had a client who, for some reason, turned him on sexually. His primary process was to maintain his persona as an analyst, but his secondary process, his sexuality, was heading in a different direction. I said to him, 'Use your beginner's mind. What's it like to have a stiff penis?' I assumed he knew nothing at all about sexuality. He laughed and, to my surprise, told me a joke. He said, 'When you want to sleep with a woman, you go to her and say, "Let's get something straight between us!"' He meant the penis, of course! So I said, 'Go and tell her that you want to get something straight.' With some trepidation he did as I said and was quite surprised when she confessed a secret. 'So you know all about it,' she said and, to his shock and relief, proceeded to tell him all about a love affair with another man that she had been hiding from him.

SYMPTOMS AND SIGNALS

As you see, proprioception can tell you a lot about the people around you. I remember an interesting proprioceptive signal I had when an analysand told me that he had to go to the hospital for an examination. We talked and worked on his body problem. I was convinced that there was nothing organically wrong with him. Actually, I refused to believe that there could be something seriously wrong. As soon as he left, I had a violent attack of diarrhea. My body was telling me that I was 'scared shitless,' that I knew this man was seriously ill and about to die, but I was afraid. My problem was that I followed his primary process which told me that with belief in magical healers, God, or a divine spirit physical disease would disappear. I did not have the guts to tell him that I really believed that physical disease is not something God should take away. In fact, I believed, and still do now, that disease is actually God's message to us, a dream revealing our totality.

Consider the following situation. A group of seminar participants are eating breakfast. One person, Bea, is eating slowly and simultaneously being bothered by her neighbor, Irene, who wants to know about Bea's dream. Bea gets a headache while talking to Irene. Later in the day, during the seminar work, Bea re-enacted the breakfast scene because she still had her headache. As she felt her headache, she expressed its proprioceptive signal with her hand as a pinching, pressing motion. She looked at her hand and realized what it was doing: pressing people. She then began to press people around her. When she got to Irene, she pressed, and *ex*pressed the verbal statement behind the motion: 'I am not satisfied with you. You hide behind a mask and never come out with what you want to say.' As soon as this proprioceptive signal was realized, Bea's headache went away, but Irene arrived at her edge, which was to defend herself. The two women began to wrestle and suddenly Bea remembered the dream Irene had once told her about a hero fighting a dragon.

Here is a good example of how a body problem can be related to the environment. Bea's proprioception, the headache and its related motion, was in part a reaction to Irene. Yet Bea's headache was almost impersonal, it was a blocked signal which belonged to the communication field, the dreambody in which she lived. It belonged to both Irene and Bea, to the breakfast table that morning.

A body symptom can be considered, at least theoretically, a statement from one aspect of a field to another, from an active to a passive part saying, 'Hey! Wake up and exist!' In this case, the headache brought both Bea and Irene out of their sweet passivity to an edge in their development. The dream field organizing the secondary process was a battle between two immense powers, the dragon and the hero, the world of normal and passive relating and the world of conscious awareness.

STIFF NECKS

The study of proprioceptive signals borders on medicine and parapsychology; symptoms are part of the total communication field. A woman once came to me complaining of a stiff neck and put her hand on her neck. When I amplified this hand motion, she imagined a spirit in her hand trying to push her to the ground. I encouraged her to continue with this fantasy and she heard this spirit say, 'I make pain in your neck and won't let you up until you bring me, the spirit of negativity, with you wherever you go.' Here again, a body symptom is a signal to the individual asking to be expressed to the collective. Thus, one way to see a body problem is as a collective dream, as a spirit in the field we live in. These spirits are asking us to be the channels for their message to the rest of the field. Thinking about our body problems in this way changes our entire attitude towards disease. We need not be so panicked and upset, we need not rush for a pill every time we feel pain. And above all, we need not feel guilty about getting sick, suspecting that we have somehow 'created it' by doing something wrong.

SPATIAL AND TEMPORAL SIGNALS

I have separated signals into their specific channels because differentiation helps train awareness in communication. Any given message may also appear in several channels at once. In addition to individual signals, there are also signals sent out by the couple as a unit which are impossible to categorize as 'his,' 'hers,' or 'theirs.' These collective or field signals will be explained in detail in a later chapter, but here I would like to mention how a few of these signals appear in the way couples and groups use space and time.

Where does one partner sit relative to the other? How far apart are they? What part of the room do they occupy? How much time does each use when talking, how much time do they give each other? A woman who confided to me that she was very weak and could never assert herself talked non-stop about herself until I pointed out to her that non-stop talking was a form of assertion. An example of a spatial signal concerns a man who had leukemia and insisted that he wasn't ready to give up, he was too interested in life. Yet I noticed that he was sitting very close to the door of my practice. I guessed at the meaning of this and asked him if, in spite of his insistence that he wanted to live, he did not notice some tendency in his life to step out of difficult situations. He then told me of several suicide attempts which followed apparently unsolvable difficulties in his life. Our work then focused on how to solve his present problems. If this man feels he cannot work out his difficulties, then leukemia will simply be another method of stepping out of a given time and space.

ON SIGNAL STUDY

I have mentioned a few of the most common and important human signals. My list encompasses probably one percent of the total human capacity to communicate. I want to stress that learning about the variety of signals is important, but not as important as learning how to pick them up. Therefore, this book is not a list of human signals, but rather a text which prompts the reader to discover why it is he notices some signals but misses others. Signal study occurs, again and again, every time you have a relationship conflict, every time you do not understand your partner, enemy, child, or every time you feel misunderstood by someone else. This beginning is accompanied by the humbling realization that we have blocks of some signals and processes. Therefore, the beginning of signal study is simultaneously the discovery of your own limitations and edges in communication.

Chapter 6
EDGES

Within every relationship problem lies our mysterious way of filtering out some information and picking up other information from our environment. These filters freeze communication; they make it static and rigid as opposed to changing and fluid. Furthermore, people are generally unconscious of the way they filter out their own memories, scenes, words, and feelings from awareness. For example, think of a child playing. He is having a great time, completely absorbed in his game. But at one point he gets distracted and loses his concentration. He moves his legs in an erratic, incomprehensible manner. Finally, he jumps up from what he's doing and runs to the bathroom. Urinating and playing were in conflict. The child was identified with his playing and was disidentified from his body, from his physical urge to urinate. Intentions and secondary processes were incongruent so he sent out double signals.

IDENTITY CRISIS
Double signals point to an edge which is splitting off the message of the secondary process. Each double signal creates an identity crisis, it antagonizes the ego which has identified itself with the primary process. An edge forms a definition of oneself and comprises the boundaries of consciousness. It is always associated with ideas, with deep-seated belief systems, with personal identity, with a life philosophy about who one really is. Together with every double signal comes an implicit edge which could well turn

out to be the greatest mystery in psychology. In the instance of the parson's wife I mentioned earlier, her edge is the belief that it is wrong to flirt or to show needs. Thus, her needs and flirtatious behavior go underground and resurface in the form of the night club singer. They come out in her clothing and make her, like all of us, a split personality.

The boy, unaware of his urge to urinate, is a classic example of children's edges. Look at the drawings of little children. There are only heads at first, then later arms and feet are added, and finally chest and bellies. A child identifies himself with his ideas and not with his body. Young children typically have an edge against their body and its somatic and proprioceptive signals such as urinating and fatigue.

BREAKTHROUGHS

It's important to realize that just bringing up double signals is only part of our task. It is relieving, it clarifies and fluidifies relationships, but it is not enough. For if the primary process has not come into conscious conflict with the secondary process, if the edge separating the two has not been worked on, the split will form again and the same internal troubles and conflicts will occur again.

For the parson's wife, expressing her shadow won't suffice, even encouraging her to flirt won't be enough. She has to find out for herself what her inner attitude and prejudice toward the night club singer is. It's necessary and meaningful to debate with herself, and no amount of understanding, coaxing, or willpower will enable her to cross the edge without 'having it out' with her own inner belief system.

EDGES AND DREAMS

In order to find your own edges, take a look at the dreams you had last night, or ask yourself, What could I never express verbally to my partner? What internal images frighten me? What scenes am I stopping from happening because I'm convinced it would be disastrous? What body sensation do I abhor? What posture or position could I not possibly make? There it is, a list of edges which help to split you up and a list of edges which serve as an introduction to your dreams. Dreams happen just over the edge of what we are able to do. Dream figures are the parts of us which are beyond our awareness, located on the other side of our edge. Edges also serve as a guide to our body symptoms, double signals, and body problems. Dream work alone isn't enough. Asking people to live parts of their dreams won't work because the edge against these parts has not been sufficiently taken into consideration.

EDGES AND ILLNESS

Illness and disease always seem to occur right on people's edges. If you need to work verbally with people on a body symptom because they are shy about body work, you might try an experiment. Ask what it is that they just can't do, what is the most difficult and frightening thing for them to imagine. If you were to challenge them and say, 'Yes, I'm sure you have the creativity to go ahead and do this,' their reaction would indicate how their edge is linked to their symptom. Touching upon an edge amplifies the experience of a symptom. Working around the edge can make a symptom appear, worsen, heal, or even disappear! Even an old, broken bone which has healed improperly can suddenly start to hurt again.

I remember working with a man and a woman in a relationship workshop. As the woman got to the crucial point, the edge in the work, she said, 'And I'm just sure that I can't live without you.' All of a sudden a mild rash which she had had broke out so violently that welts appeared. She realized what she had just said, worked on her edge, and afterwards could say that it wasn't true anymore, she could live without him and intended to do so! Five minutes later, her welts had disappeared. What happened to this woman? She had grabbed on to the man because she believed the world would end if she were alone. She believed she was utterly incapable of standing alone, and this belief cut her off from her own strength and capabilities. That's when her rash appeared, as a somatized double signal of strength. Her edge made her feel like a weak female who needed someone to lean on and split off her power which came back as a rash.

A similar case I had concerned a troubled couple who came to see me. The man had very itchy skin. He walked in simultaneously itching and scratching and said that as far as he was concerned, he had no trouble at all with his wife. Later in the session, he said that he was a weak man who couldn't express himself because his mother had emasculated him. His weakness prevented him from changing, he explained to me. His edge was his hypnotic belief in his own weakness. I challenged this belief and told him that if he was strong enough to trouble his wife, he was strong enough to express himself. He then got terribly angry at me and at his wife. He yelled at us both and stopped itching. His skin irritation was somatized anger that had gotten 'edged' out by his lack of faith in himself. Once again, this skin irritation was linked to the relationship. His wife confessed that she was afraid of hurting his feelings. Her fears of hurting him contributed to his troubles. The husband and wife were mirror images of each other. She was a weakling for not being direct with him and he was a weakling for accepting her behavior. Their relationship dreambody consisted of secondary aggression and primary mothering, and the edge in this dreambody was against being direct and definitive.

EDGES AND COLLIDING MYTHS

Edges and their associated double signals behave like borders between countries. Thus, tinkering with the edge tinkers with borderline conflicts, psychosomatic ailments, and, above all, the myths belonging to the two different countries. The problem is that there is no flow of communication between the lands. The parts which are separated are strangers to each other.

For example, the part of the woman who was independent and the part which was dependent do not know each other. The part of the couple above which is violent and the part which sweetly abides by the status quo are separated. The reason why it is so difficult to bring up double signals and work on psychosomatic symptoms is that the myths of the two countries are different. In one 'country' people believe that women need men, in another, the myth of the Amazon, of warrior-like women prevails. In one country goodwill and Christianity may reign while in the other the Darwinian rule of survival of the fittest reigns. These are some of our colliding myths.

THE FUNCTION OF UNCONSCIOUSNESS

In certain situations the edge is so strong that it becomes virtually impossible to make the individual aware of anything but the myth the edge protects. I once worked with a therapist and her client who had run into an impasse because the client had fallen in love with the therapist. The therapist feared losing herself in sexual contact with the client. The therapist complained that the client always wanted to remain after the session was over; apparently she had an edge to being more disciplined. She got over this edge by saying to her client, 'Your time is up, stop gloating and staring at me, and say something direct!' Once one person in a couple crosses an edge, the other is forced to do so as well. This client, however, just stayed there and looked dreamily into the space between the two women. Why didn't she react or hear the therapist's definiteness? Why was she still hoping that the therapist would be her lover when everything pointed against it?

I decided to take the client's side and act out for her what I saw. 'I refuse to pick up any information,' I said, 'which is going to interrupt my trance. As long as I am in my trance I can fantasize about eternally sensitive love, about mythical joy, nirvana, and heavenly peace. I never want to give up this fantasy because my life will come to an end if I do.' This guess about her signal did it. She burst into tears and I told her she needed to complete that fantasy. I recommended that she write a fairy tale and find out what meaning the fairy tale could have for her. At that moment she was happy because she felt understood.

When the therapist went over the edge, the client stayed

firmly implanted and behaved as if she did not hear the negative feedback from her therapist. She had an edge against being negative herself and against hearing negativity. Hence, her sweet primary process kept all negative secondary processes out of conscious awareness. The function of this type of unconsciousness is that it protected her primary process, her drive and need for love so that it could fulfill and complete itself in legendary or mythical form. Only when this myth is completed will the client be able to perceive and consciously send out negative or aggressive signals. Until that point she is locked into a mythical world which asks for her understanding and appreciation. The edge protects myths; when the edge cannot be jumped or when people are unable to perceive the reality of their partners, the edge is there to protect and to preserve the unconsciousness until it is fully completed.

TRAGIC ASPECTS OF UNCONSCIOUSNESS

A tragedy accompanies the necessary and positive aspect of unconsciousness surrounding edges. Consider a quiet, introverted man working on a relationship with a more extraverted woman who is able to express a lot of feeling. As he speaks softly, sitting back in his chair, she leans forward with loving eyes, asking again and again what he is thinking and feeling. His posture and language say that he needs to be very quiet, in fact he refuses to express himself, especially upon demand. She continues to lean forward, requesting both verbally and nonverbally more interaction with him.

I asked her how long she was going to continue looking at him, imagining that he would one day give her what she wanted. Immediately she said, 'My god, I've just spent thirty years hoping he would be what he is not, why am I doing this?' After a moment's reflection, she explained that she was still trying to get her quiet father, who had died when she was still a little girl, to relate to her and love her.

When I asked her partner how long he was going to sit there passively, imagining she would one day leave him in peace, the function of his unconsciousness about her came out. 'I am dreaming,' he said, 'that one day my mother is going to stop nagging me to be nice to her!'

Such insights are moments in relationship work when partners seem to wake up. They realize that they are dreaming, that their eyes and ears are filled with dreams, that they are not seeing, hearing or feeling the signals of the people they are communicating with but are looking at ancient dreams, imagining that their partners are like these dreams, even when they are not. These are moments when the focus of relationship turns to each individual. At a moment like this, one can put a piece of paper in between the people so that each may project more freely and see exactly what images they are projecting. The tragedy is that a couple's unconsciousness prevents them from knowing, loving and communicating with each other. One way out, however, is to dream on until the fantasy or dream completes itself and changes.

EDGES TO PRIMARY AND TO SECONDARY PROCESSES

Another reason for the enigmatic inability of people to make the most obvious personality developments is because many edges are little, tiny ones which go unnoticed because they're overshadowed by the more obvious, immense edges. A really sweet man can't develop his manliness, not just because he has an edge against his manliness, but also because he hates recognizing how sweet he is! In process language we say there is a little edge, a barrier to the primary process and a larger, more obvious edge between the primary process and the secondary process.

Take the case of the typical, mild-mannered couple who say that they realize they are too sweet and tame and would like to connect to instinctive, expressive, and more colorful energy but simply cannot. When working with this couple, the first thing to notice is that they are extremely well-mannered. Even though they admit to this behavior, they are unaware of how it functions and how it looks. They don't see how their simplest gestures reflect this extreme well-manneredness. They don't realize that being decent and motherly to one another can be seen in the way both sit patiently, listening with their heads cocked an inch to the left in an 'understanding' fashion and waiting politely for the other one to finish talking. Working with them on this posture demonstrated that it represented the 'well-mannered mother' they were trying to get rid of. They need to realize that even inquiring as to the well-being of one another, playing therapist, and being understanding and helpful is a form of this mothering and can be destructive if this solicitude is not genuine or if it negates other, more impatient feelings.

The first step to take with this couple is to amplify their mothering. Of course this would immediately constellate the first edge. Explaining to them that they have been being motherly all along would help them get over the first edge. In order for this couple to be more direct and energetically involved with each other, they have to first become aware of the 'mother.'

This mother process is actually patterned in the dream of one member of this couple. The man dreamed that he had to move into his mother's bed and then all would be in order! In other words, he had to get into the role of mothering. They both have to do *more* of what is already, unconsciously happening between them. Then afterwards, they could move the mother out, but only by consciously taking over the mother's role in the relationship, instead of being unconsciously directed by it. They do not connect to their wildness because their mothering needs to be appreciated first.

Now it's easy to see why I have divided processes into primary and secondary and have left the words 'conscious' and 'unconscious' aside. The primary process is also a bit unconscious. Even though people talk about it, they are still not completely aware of it. Primary signals are usually cultural processes which have become so automatic that no one takes the time and patience to get down to their roots and discover how they're manifested. If this hasn't been done, it is naturally impossible to get to the next, deeper process and what lies behind it.

DOUBLE AND TRIPLE SIGNALS

Once the mother edge has been crossed, an edge against expression or instincts comes up, and after that, the next edge. Once the first gate and its demon is passed, there is always another one to pass through. Beyond each edge, you proceed deeper and deeper into individuality as a person and as a couple. Edges are like mirages, constantly challenging you to move over them and revealing the many dimensions of relationship as you live on.

Thus, there's quite an involved message behind even a simple statement such as, 'I am too conventional and want to change.' There is the 'I' responsible for awareness of the conventionality. There is the conventional person and the accompanying signal of decency, and then there is the third signal, the unconventional person already implicit in the desire to change. There is an edge between the 'I' and the 'conventional one' and a greater, more awesome edge between the 'conventional one' and the 'future person.' It seems to me at this point that the key to the entire personality of an individual and of a couple lies in appreciating edges, the function of the unconsciousness they create, and the value of the myths colliding on each side of the barrier.

Chapter 7
COUPLE'S SIGNALS

In previous chapters I discussed the channels, signals, and edges characterizing individuals in relationships. In this chapter I want to discuss the couple or family as a unit and the signals it sends out. In particular, I want to focus on the differences or incongruities frequently at the bottom of relationship problems: incongruities between what the family intends to do together and what is unintentionally happening.

PRIMARY PROCESSES
The primary process of a family is the combination of their intentions and identities. These identities often appear as a group ego or the 'we' in the sentences of the members. For example, in one family the mother may say, 'We are a family that loves to be together.' No one takes issue with this statement: hence, togetherness describes this family's primary process. By implication, separateness is a secondary process, and it's not difficult to imagine what it is that's bothering this family with two teenagers. The kids are beginning to disturb the system by wanting to be more independent.

Another family will insist, for example, that all of its members abide by a certain faith. Their religion is a primary process, one which they may be shy to admit, but one which programs and rules their communication. Rules about intermarriage, aggression, spending and earning money, and discipline are all aspects of a family's primary process.

Remember that even though the primary process is primary, i.e. close to consciousness, it's still not a fully conscious system. If the therapist misses this fact, he can insult the entire family in the first five minutes without knowing why. For example, if the therapist sees a family whose primary process is harmony, but which complains about a lack of energy and force, he will never help them by simply encouraging them to be forceful with each other. He first has to acknowledge their interest in harmony, even compliment it, and talk about anything else they're interested in. If the therapist doesn't respect the primary process and its edges, he will end up irritated and frustrated by the family's apparent resistance to change.

REASONS FOR COMING
A central manifestation of the primary process is the reason people come to the therapist. There are innumerable reasons why people enter therapy. Regardless of the therapist's opinions about the reasons, they are important to the client and must be considered. The central issues for pairs are extramarital relationships, sexual 'abnormalities,' breaking up or divorce, boredom, lack of energy, and the need for independence, to name just a few. A typical issue for young families is the sick child who has strange and unusual symptoms no doctor can treat. He steals, masturbates, refuses to eat, or is diagnosed insane. Family therapists call the sick or 'bad' one in the family the 'identified patient' in order to emphasize that he is not the only patient, but one member of a troubled family. It is important to remember that the patient is the problem upon which the family focuses and therefore the primary process for the family. If the therapist insists too quickly upon the secondary process, he will upset the family and sometimes even the 'patient.'

In fact, if the therapist ignores the primary process because he identifies the deeper, unconscious problem of the family, the family will leave. I have seen many people leave their therapist because the therapist never considered their reason for coming. For example, one couple told me that they left their previous family therapist because he never dealt with the reason for coming: the husband's impotence. When I heard that, I decided to get right down to business. 'Well,' I said, 'let me see directly what you do together in bed. At least stand up and hug each other. Let's work directly on body contact.' So they both stood up, a bit self-consciously, and acted as if they were embracing. Suddenly the wife stopped and said, 'Ha! That's just the problem. I always get into bed with him because he tells me to. I do it even though I don't want to and secretly hope that he'll realize it.' He said, 'Well *that's* why I always get turned off with you, you're really never quite there, and I feel it.'

BEING FOOLED BY THE PRIMARY PROCESS

There are many situations in which the individual or family act as if they've come for help, but their secondary processes are stronger than the admitted primary ones. You need only imagine the irate husband who is dragged into therapy because the wife wants him to change, or the little kid who appears before the therapist's door because a possessive and overanxious father is concerned about the boy's colds. The therapist shouldn't assume that people come because they need help. Many come because they need someone to beat up, some are looking for a weak therapist to overcome in hopes of becoming strong. Others come to form a coalition with the therapist against the partner, not to seek growth or help. Still others come in order to be nourished; they are looking for a parent, not an analyst.

I remember once being trapped by a family whom I had called in because I thought that they would be able to help their ill daughter. Naturally, they complied, but they merely wanted to put her in an institution and were not the least bit interested in understanding her. I called them to see me, then I foolishly assumed that their presence was a sign that they wanted to change! Finally, to make things worse, I did my best to change them, and was disappointed because they would not follow my recommendations! If I had been smart enough to ask why they had come, I could have saved myself a lot of trouble. I would have realized that their primary process consisted of listening and following foolish therapists like myself, while their secondary process was to push their child to grow up and get out of the house!

People need a lot of time to feel at home with a therapist. They need to involve him in their primary process and feel that he respects their identities as individuals. Furthermore, the therapist must understand that double signals are part of an unconscious dreaming system. Working too quickly with secondary processes challenges these identities and can be harmful if it is done before an ordinary conscious rapport is established.

THE COLLECTIVITY OF THE SECONDARY PROCESSES

Asking one member of a family a question frequently evokes a response from another. One way of looking at this would be to assume that people are weak, stupid, and allow others to talk for them. Another, more process-oriented view would be to see it as an indication that the entire family operates as a single unit; one person is the mouth, another is the heart, and the other is the legs.

Take the example of Alex. If I ask his mother who stole the cookies, and Alex turns red, I can see that the problem bothers not only the mother, but Alex as well. Or, I can ask Alex who stole the cookies and should not be surprised if the father burps. He, too, has something to confess. When father finally begins to talk about stealing, Alex's sister, Marie, begins to fidget, and in this moment, she becomes the secondary process wanting to enter the scene. She tells us that she thinks everyone in the family is guilty of something. Such loud laughter follows this statement, that I ask everyone to talk about their guilt. The stories finally come out, and the weight comes off Alex's shoulders for being the only thief in the family. The whole family was guilty of doing 'forbidden' things.

COUPLE'S SIGNALS

If we watch an entire family discussing a particular topic, the giggles, motions, or fidgeting in one body, or part of one's body carry the secondary process for the entire group at that moment. These unintended signals together with the topic of conversation create the family process. Thus, working with an individual's signals in a group setting works simultaneously with the individual's and family's process. One couple told me that they were open about their feelings. But the husband sat with his head down and shoulders hunched, and the little boy sat alone in the corner. Both parents were upset with the boy's introversion. I told the child to pull away even further, and everyone got nervous as the entire family arrived at an edge. The child cried and said that everyone wanted him to show his feelings all the time, and he thought this requirement was insensitive! The two extraverted parents had to learn that real feeling sometimes means withdrawing and being quiet. The child's position in space and the father's head withdrawn into his shoulders were double signals, secondary processes for a family which had intended to be direct and open about everything.

TERRITORIAL SIGNALS

Everyone is aware of space. Think of your own family or the one you grew up in. One member of a family is frequently absent. Consider the possibility that he is the unconscious part of the group body. When all members are present, each has a special place to sleep, each has a place at the collective dining table. Who sits where? Does the father sit at the head or in the corner? Where is the mother? And which child sits where? One effective way of working with spatial signals is to amplify the space between people. If two are close, ask them to be closer. If one is sitting by himself at the end of the table near the door, ask him to move further away. The extremes in time and space, the one closest to the door, the two closest together describe the unconscious situation of the entire family.

In one family I worked with, the mother and daughter sat very close at the table. When I asked them to get even closer they immediately acknowledged that they do this in coalition against the father and brother who were cold and feelingless. But this lack of feeling bothered everyone; the father and brother also complained that the two women were hard and cold. The whole family suffered from the problem which arose by amplifying the sitting positions.

WORKING IN THE FAMILY SPACE

It's also possible to amplify by forbidding spatial signals. For example, one couple arrived at my practice saying they wanted to understand each other, but sat far apart and looked away from each other. When I asked them to reverse the signal, to sit next to each other, she said she was scared of him and wanted to avoid him. He said that his problems had nothing to do with her, despite the fact that they had come to see me to work on their relationship. I naturally recommended that they follow their strong secondary processes and avoid each other, not even think about each other for at least a week. I encouraged them to work on themselves, alone, and try to understand their own situation as well as possible. He argued with me, saying he loved her. So I switched, recommended they pay more attention to one another. They were both happy with me (for understanding their primary process) and decided later to part in friendship. The way people sit is a deep and powerful structure in relationship.

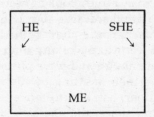

MORE ABOUT GROUP SIGNALS

Thus what people say, the issues they come with, and the statements they make are group primary processes. All the unintentional statements and signals are secondary. People's sitting arrangement is normally secondary, except when the positions are intentionally created, for example in religious rituals where the sitting positions are deliberately organized according to the consensus belief system. Where sitting and standing positions are willfully organized, secondary processes appear spatially in the direction the people sit and face or spatially in terms of WHO is sitting WHERE. There are many other fascinating group signals such as the size and age of a group, its position in a given culture, and its rate of growth or deterioration. In this book, I will concentrate mainly on spatial signals because they have great practical importance in family work.

DIVORCING SPACE

A couple recently came to see me. He sat next to her, though he said that he was afraid to do so. She simply looked in the other direction when he sat down but did not move. They said that they were in the midst of a divorce and had come to see if they could work things out. Their primary process was to work out the details of their divorce, but their secondary process consisted of the directions they were facing. They sat together in order to 'work things out.' So I asked them to work on the way they were facing. 'Look away from him,' I said to her. This did not work. Thinking I could forbid her signal, I said, 'look at him.' That did it. Out poured all of her hatred towards him. He brought out his antagonism towards her and they both decided then and there they did not want to make any more effort to work it out. They had tried enough and were now ready to part and leave the rest up to their lawyer.

OTHER EXAMPLES

In the following examples I want to condense the material in order to focus upon territorial signals and processes. Each square represents the room where I practice. I will designate 'Pa' for father, 'Ma' for mother, 'b' for boy, and 'g' for girl. 'Gpa' and 'Gma' are grandfather and grandmother, respectively. The following scenes arose when I asked the family or couple to arrange the sitting positions themselves and to organize the hour the way they wanted to. The meaning of the positions unfolded as a result of amplifying, forbidding, or acting out the signals.

THE CHILD IS 'SICK'

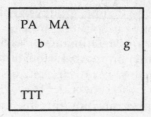

In the room to the right there is the coalition between the father, mother, and son in one corner. On the other side of the room, all alone, sits the girl. The arrangement shows three therapists, three because we are weak and in need of strength against the 'enemy' who will not change as we want! The little girl is alone, she carries the secondary process for the whole family. One of the therapists, the one on the far right, sides strongly with the girl. The girl is catatonic, so 'sensitive' she can barely speak. The other family members hate her and only want to put her in a hospital. Their sitting positions show that they oppose the therapists who all believe that the family should change.

After gathering information about primary processes, how could we work with these spatial signals? We could amplify the territorial message by asking the girl to move even further away or for the therapists to oppose and challenge the family more. Or, we could do the opposite and have the girl sit in the midst of the family, breaking apart their coalition. This latter method would bring the implicit family tension quickly to the foreground.

FATHER IS HATED
Consider the following set up. The father has just come home from prison. We can read from the spatial signals that he faces a coalition: the mother and the two children, all

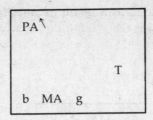

avoiding the father. The father feels terrible about this. I encouraged the father to move further into the corner and he immediately began to cry. He said he felt rejected and ostracized by the whole world. His wife and children expressed their anger at him for his bad behavior. He begged them to help him with his problems. Surprisingly, they decided to help out. At the end of the session, this family dreambody looked like this:

```
┌─────────────────────────────┐
│                             │
│  PA  b                      │
│  MA  g                      │
│                             │
│                             │
│                             │
│                        T    │
│                             │
└─────────────────────────────┘
```

FAMILY WITH CHILDREN

```
┌─────────────────────────────┐
│                    b ↗       │
│                             │
│      PA→  ←MA               │
│      b→  ←  g               │
│                             │
│          T                  │
└─────────────────────────────┘
```

The next example is a family in which the parents have trouble making boundaries between themselves and their small children. As a result their relationship has become strained and tense. In fact, they frequently argue about how to bring up the kids. It is for this reason that the mother and father are facing each other, each using the child of the same sex as reinforcement of their position. It was so difficult for me to work with them that after a while I sent the kids into my waiting room. As soon as I did, the fight between the parents that had been simmering in the background erupted. It was only possible for the parents to have a relationship when they were forced to stop using the children as a buffer. The field of this family is the typical field of a family with small children.

THE BLACK SHEEP

In the next example, father and daughter sit together, and they both consider mother impossible. She is undoubtedly the unconscious for this family unit. She wants to do her own thing and is not very interested in family life.

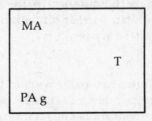

Thus, the father has become the mother and lover of the daughter. One could either encourage the mother to move further off, or to come closer to the father. I did the latter, and she admitted that she did not like him for particular reasons. I was shocked when the daughter agreed with her and asked her father to change! The child had been the medium of expression between the adults whose communication had been disturbed.

NO BOUNDARIES

The couple below sit on the couch together. They act very warm and loving to one another but are bothered by the fact that there is no boundary between them.

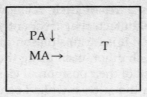

They both have difficulty being definitive about their feelings. I chose to ask them to get even closer together and an explosion occurred! The creation of boundaries began. Of course, I could have also worked with the body gestures. She sat next to him but faced me. He sat near her, and half faced us both. She was implying with her double signal that she wanted to be nice to him, but simultaneously wanted distance from him and needed my help to do so.

Creating distance and making boundaries in order to do your own thing is a widespread problem, one which is often at the bottom of so-called impotence and frigidity. If you do not consciously make boundaries in the relationship, you turn off or you turn your partner off with double signals that say, 'Stay away, this is my territory!'

HEROIN
The next picture shows two older women figures in a family protecting the youngest member, who is addicted to heroin. I used this arrangement by asking the protecting figures to protect the youngest even more and enter into her life.

```
      MA  g  MA
       →     ←
          T
```

The youngest had left the nest years ago, and I asked the older women to take more responsibility for the girl's life and help her kick her habit. They agreed, and I found out later that she had subsequently kicked her habit.

ALCOHOL AND RESIGNATION

The spatial situation below shows a man facing me, discussing many problems which he asked to work on. The woman is leaning back. Suddenly he mentions the word 'alcohol' and I notice that she leans further back on her hands.

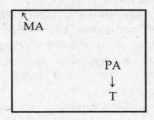

I tell her to move further away and to lie down. After a while, she moves forward again and says she's tired of giving up on his alcohol problem. His position facing me was a way of avoiding her anger, which he suspected might result in divorce. I encouraged them to divorce right then and there, and to have it out about the alcohol problem. She became very forceful, and he was genuinely touched and wanted to change. His addiction was part of a field in which giving up and avoiding conflicts were secondary processes.

WHO IS TO BLAME?

Let's make a 'time-line' of a day starting in the morning (8 am) and moving downward to the evening. Look at the way the family below uses time.

```
8 am     ⎫⎫
         ⎬⎬  MA
         ⎭
12 pm    ⎫   g
         ⎬   b
9 pm     ⎭⎫
         ⎬⎬  PA
10 pm     ⎭⎭
```

Ma is home in the morning, Pa from 9 to 10 at night, the kids are around all day. In the session, father was attacked by mother for not being around much. When he admitted his reasons for being away and his negativity towards the family, the air cleared and the family was relieved. But according to the diagram, the wife was not around much either. When she admitted that she never wanted the family in the first place, the problem which was originally the father's ended up belonging to mother, as well. I recommended the family get a 'mother's helper,' which seemed to relieve everyone, to begin with at least.

FAMILY WITH TEENAGERS
Here is the time plan of a family with teenage children.

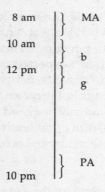

Ma is home from 8 to 10 a.m., and no one is around at the same time. Yet each was blaming the other for not being 'with the family.' After I made the diagram and showed it to the family, they all confessed that they wanted to grow out of the family. The parents were in the midst of a mid-life crisis, and needed to do their own thing. The kids were growing up and were ready to say that they wanted to be adults and have responsibility for their own lives.

KIDS AND PARENTS
Kids often carry the secondary process for the family in a very direct way. I remember one little boy sent to see me by

his pediatrician because his chronic bronchitis and bouts of pneumonia responded poorly to medication. I decided to see the whole family together. They sat down, father and child in one corner, mother in another. The child continuously coughed. I asked the father to move closer to the mother and immediately an incredible and painful story came out. The mother was overcome nightly by attacks of paranoia and tried to strangle the father. As the father told the story, the little boy, who apparently knew nothing of these nocturnal scenes, sat there shocked, his eyes wide open, staring silently at his mother without coughing. In this family, the mother's insanity, the father's weak way of dealing with it, and the child's choking sensations were all tied together.

CHILDHOOD ASTHMA

In another family system, the little child was suffering from severe and potentially lethal asthma. I first met the family in a seminar setting, and it was apparent that the parents were too decent to each other and had an edge against being direct and aggressive. Throughout the entire seminar their child was completely at ease with the setting and had no hesitation to play during the sessions. During one session in which I was working with someone else, he jumped into the middle and began to protect the person I was working with. He put his little hands over my nose and mouth in an attempt to cut off my wind.

This behavior is very significant. Asthma sufferers I have worked with all experience their symptoms as if something or someone were choking them. With the boy, I reversed the roles and acted like the asthma-maker, cutting off his air. At first he was stunned, but then, slowly but surely, he raised his little arms into the air, resisted me, and yelled, 'Superman!!' His asthma behaved like a challenger, trying to provoke his masculine spirit, his inner 'Superman power.' The child needed the asthma to stimulate his masculine energy because the family system he lived in tended to repress dramatic challenges and heroic feats.

A NOTE OF CAUTION
Young parents (and even some older ones) reading these paragraphs are certain to jump to the conclusion that if only they were whole and individuated, their children would never be ill. I think a word of warning may be in order for such parents. Children's diseases are not 'caused' by a given family situation. A very similar system may, under the same circumstances, be connected with either different symptoms or none at all. The child, like the adult, is an individual and comes with a specific heritage which predisposes him to certain diseases and protects him from certain outer circumstances as well. Thus, a given disease may fit a family system perfectly without being caused by it. Working on the family's unconscious processes may relieve the symptoms but may not alter the child's own predispositions and process of growth.

LEARNING FROM THE CHILDREN
Certainly one of the most interesting aspects of dreambody work with children is the way children reflect the unknown in the family. Take the case of a relatively ordinary family who came to see me. The mother felt that she was the bad one in the family; she had to make the rules and be the authority who was rejected by the kids.

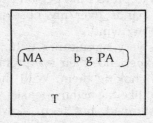

I saw from their sitting arrangement that what she was saying was accurate. She sat alone at one end of a large couch and the father and the kids sat at the other end. The mother and her rules seemed to be the secondary process for this group.

At first I encouraged one of the children to express her

antagonistic feelings towards her mother and the rules. It turned out, however, that these kids were not against rules; they wanted to be able to make them themselves! This even made the parents happy, especially when they made rules about watching television and cleaning up.

As the work proceeded, I used the children's good mood to make a play. I asked them to act out exactly how they experienced their parents. The kids demonstrated the worst moment of the day; when the father came home, he was tired and didn't want to be disturbed by the kids. However, when the kids played the homecoming scene, everyone was surprised because the kids did not portray the real father, but an angry, roaring father who yelled and screamed for peace and quiet. And what's more, this father was stingy and had no money for anyone. The real father, watching the play, defended himself and said that he was really a nice guy; he was neither stingy nor mean.

What happened here was that the kids acted out the secondary process for the father. They portrayed not how he acted, but how he unconsciously felt. They picked up his double signals, and taught him a lesson about his real self! I asked the father to learn from his teachers and be more definitive with the family, and say 'no' more often. He willingly agreed, actually relieved to be able to set down some rules. This family integrated their secondary process, the mother, by learning to be more definitive with each other.

FAMILY MYTHS
The therapist may also ask a couple or family about the first dreams, fantasies, or events that happened around the time of their original meeting or at the birth of their first child. Or, the therapist could ask about any big, accidental events which occurred at a significant moment in their relationship. Each couple has its own stories. Lovers tell about their secret rendezvous. Married couples talk about their car blowing up en route to the wedding or the tuxedo that fell in the mud. Other couples tell about their parents fighting and arguing at the wedding. Homosexual couples speak of their war with the world. All these stories are important dreams,

mythical patterns which often, perhaps always, foretell and explain the meaning of problems which occur years later.

Using early dreams and incidents as potential patterns is frequently very relieving for people, especially when relationships are in a crisis phase. I recall one couple who were having great problems. She looked down at the floor and barely replied each time he said he wanted to work on the relationship. They kept a big distance between them; this distance seemed to be the secondary process, the process of separateness. I worked with her looking down by putting a blanket between them so that they could not see each other. She said, 'What are you doing that for?' and I said, 'Tell me.' She immediately moved all the way across the room and said she wanted a divorce. He was upset and protested. I then asked about their original dreams and memories. She said that she dreamed shortly after their first meeting that he shot her in the vagina and killed her. He remembered only that they had decided not to make love the first night they spent together. When asked about those memories and dreams, I said that she experienced him as being dangerous and that he experienced the relationship with certain reservations. Somehow, the dream and memory gave them an objective pattern which had been plaguing their primary process of togetherness. They both decided in friendship, but with some reservations, to investigate the possibility of a separation.

THE I CHING

Another means of ascertaining the process of a couple is by consulting the *I CHING*. A couple at war over the traditional values of family life pulls the hexagram 'Revolution' which speaks of change conflicting with tradition. Another couple blocked over recurring difficulties pulls 'Youthful Folly,' which says that the wise man gently removes himself from recurring stupidity and awaits change which happens of itself. This couple could not give up its stupidity until a big change happened.

The amazing thing about early dreams, fantasies, events, and the *I CHING* hexagrams is that they all can be guessed by asking the couple what their edges are. Ask, 'What can you almost not do with your partner, what can you not speak about or not do with him or her?' The edges, coupled with the primary process, help reveal the overall process and governing myth behind the individual and his relationships.

In this chapter we have seen how secondary processes may be carried not only by the double signals of the individual involved in a group but also by the seating arrangement and direction they are facing. I have also indicated how the *I CHING* and early dreams may reveal secondary processes. Children at play carry these elemental processes as well. The importance of these processes becomes apparent when we recall that the problems plaguing families can often be solved by reference to secondary phenomena.

Chapter 8
WORKING WITH COUPLES

The following couple in their late fifties came to see me because of their long-standing difficulties. She is a psychologist and claims to be fed up with his jealousy. He says he's not jealous, but that she won't relate to him. In his opinion, she doesn't love him.

After they enter my office, she sits back looking smug and professional. He is dressed like a business man. She tells me that he does not admit his resistance to her. I tell her to say this to him. He responds that he does not know what she is talking about; he has no resistances. I reformulate the question and ask him if there is anything which he cannot talk to her about. With this question, I am looking for the edges which keep them separated from their dream field. He hesitates, then admits that he cannot talk about painful subjects with her because he feels she's not interested.

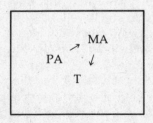

They are both obviously on their best behavior; in fact, their positions give the impression of highly intelligent people drifting emotionally apart. After listening to them intellectualize and attribute blame, I watch them draw away from each other and so I separate them emotionally to work with them individually. I ask him if he had any dreams recently. He tells me he dreamed about a dying man who won't tell anyone that he knows he's dying. We all agree that this is probably a part of himself in great pain. The projection is that he thinks *she* will not be interested in his pain. 'Pain about what?' I ask him.

He tells me that it is very difficult for him to admit that he has a wife with a career who is not there for him when he needs her. He looks down at the floor and says that without her full attention he cannot live. With this he begins to cry. She is listening to everything very quietly and then turns her body towards me, still looking at her husband. I tell her to follow what her body is trying to do, noticing that his getting over an edge brings her to one, too. I ask her to turn entirely towards me. She hesitantly says that she doesn't want to get emotional, she doesn't want any tension. She says she has had so many arguments with him that she is utterly hopeless about their relationship. She no longer wants to get upset and isn't interested in pain.

I tell her to say this directly to him, namely, that her double signals indicate that she wants no trouble. Tell him that what he projects – that she cannot speak about pain – is true! And I tell him to repeat to her that he too does not want to talk about pain, he'd prefer to die silently. Consciously focusing on avoiding pain quickly brings about the opposite. She screams and yells that he is power crazy, and he yells back that she is yelling at him. After a long and emotional exchange, she quiets down and asks me if she can consult the *I CHING* about herself. She gets number 39, 'Obstruction.' The lines speak of a great man who would like to disappear from the world, but the way is blocked and he must return to help people in adversity.

She tells me that this fits. Being a psychologist, she sees that she must return to her marriage and work things out. In fact she would prefer to work them out in herself. She gets up, not realizing that the *I CHING* recommended the opposite, namely that she 'return to the world to help,' thanks me, and walks toward the door. Suddenly her husband explodes and yells to her that even though she looks like she is taking things internally, she is really ignoring and hating him. She hesitates, admits he's right, and sits down again. He talks again about his pain and how hard 'life' is. Then all of a sudden, *he* gets up and wants to go, claiming that it is just impossible to communicate with her when she's not interested. I point out that *he* is about to leave, that he is projecting his lack of interest on to her, and recommend that he do what he is telling her to do: sit down and work on his communication. He starts to cry heavily at this point, and for the first time, she is moved by his pain, she sits next to him and puts her arms around his shoulders.

This work has several interesting points. The first one is that the man has a block to expressing his feelings and projects this upon the wife. He projects on to her the one within him who won't talk about pain, and this is reflected in the dream. But his inability to express his feelings gives him a quiet, non-demanding appearance which is the perfect excuse for her, too, to avoid difficulties.

She, however, is not merely dreamed up. The *I CHING* has told her to go into the obstructions, bear the tension, and work it out. She, too, now in her late fifties, has a problem which she shares with him: neither wants tension. Both have become hopeless and want to die. This manifests itself in the *I CHING* hexagram and in her double signals which turn away from pain.

HOPELESSNESS
Both the man and the woman have the same unconscious problem. One deals with it by putting on a persona, the other gets depressed and folds out of this world. Both have similar edges. World-weariness is characteristic of many people, especially people over fifty. But surprisingly enough there are also many young people who are hopeless and want to avoid pain, believing that nothing good can come of it.

In part, hopelessness is due to the fact that without encouragement and the right relationship tools people have no choice but to give up. They can only go so far alone. They assume that their partner cannot be changed or that change will result in greater pain or that there is no need to change their relationships. Because she is a psychologist, the woman in this couple has the added difficulty of believing she is wiser and more intelligent than her partner. She attempts to change herself without regard or reference to her partner.

INTROVERTING AS EASING TROUBLE
Hopelessness prompts people to introvert and work solely with themselves. The woman's attempt to introvert by consulting the *I CHING* angered the man and disturbed the relationship. Likewise, his desire to leave almost ruined their chances of getting together. At a certain point in a relationship, the very tendency to withdraw and reflect on what is happening can be destructive by increasing existing problems. This contradicts the idea that individual change is the highest possible good! There is a time and place for this sort of change, it is a matter of the Tao. Individual change can thus be used as an escape or as a method for avoiding pain. Introverting becomes problematic if it becomes the goal and not one phase of a relationship.

COLLECTIVE DREAMBODIES
Two empirical facts are outstanding. First, we cannot tell who is the cause and who is the effect of the problem in this example, and second, there was no solution to the problem they presented. He dreamed her up to avoid pain just as much as she dreamed him up to give up and die. Neither her initial complaint of jealousy, nor his complaint of lack of love was directly solved. These facts lead us to conclude that (a) there is no linear causality; no one person does something 'bad' to someone else, and (b) there is no one problem that needs solving. The very idea that one is wrong or that there is a problem which one day must be solved belongs to the primary process of a couple and has minimal bearing upon the emerging secondary process.

In this couple's dreambody, the primary parts which

avoid pain must learn to communicate with the double signals. All parts of the dreambody need to develop awareness as parts of a greater unity. He plays the part which masks over pain, and she plays the part no longer interested in working things out. By working on both of their edges to pain, the two of them communicate better with one another when they are together and feel better about each other when they are alone.

RUTH AND DAVID
In the following case which was taped by one of my students it becomes apparent how the members of a couple become functions of the overall process. The part transcribed here is only one part of a longer session in which many topics were considered. Ruth and David are in their later middle life and have five children. They have both been in therapy before, individually, and now as a couple. They are discussing their sexual contact which has been absent for almost a year. As the conversation begins, David is on the floor, Ruth is sitting higher up on a chair, and the therapist is sitting between them, forming a triangle.

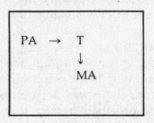

As you read, notice how difficult it is to follow the verbal content and sense of the conversation.

Therapist: So, how is it going between the two of you in your sexual life? What is missing?
Ruth: Things are a bit unerotic.
David: (irritated) Wait, things are still new, sex is just beginning.
Ruth: (with raised voice) I only said that I have been in a

hole for a week, I am depressed. I noticed that I need a lot of love, and I don't have it.

Therapist: Why not reach out to David?

Ruth: I can only do that when my partner does it, too.

David: (coughs) I cannot do everything at once.

Ruth: I can't animate him, I need someone to care for me. I want to be spoiled and not have to fight for it.

Therapist: Spoiled by him?

Ruth: Yes, from you (to David). If I cannot get my happiness, then (softly) I will go and seek another relationship. Then, (laughing) but look, even that wouldn't help. (Her voice drops.)

Therapist: How do you fantasize this affair?

Ruth: It is sad, it won't work. Yet, I see candles, and atmosphere, and a bubble bath.

Therapist: David should help you with that.

David: (clowning) I can't help with a bubble bath. (All laugh)

Ruth: (turning to David) What happens in you when I speak?

David: (ignoring her question) First I have to get rid of this cold and stop drinking (coughs).

Ruth: (continuing previous statement) The most important thing for me is love which would help me. I wish I was not like that, but what can I do?

Therapist: Ask him.

David: (coughs) Let me get over my cold first.

Therapist: (to David) What do you mean?

David: I am suffering from a fever.

Ruth: Last week you had no fever.

David: Depressed . . . (coughs again).

Ruth: My love and life are going by . . .

Therapist: Uh huh. (to David) What are your feet doing?

David: (feet jiggling) I walked into something with my shoes, I got dirty from the stairs. . . .

PRIMARY AND SECONDARY PROCESSES

I present this undramatic verbatim report because it shows numerous, typical relationship patterns. To begin with, there are two simultaneous and separate processes happening. The primary process is the discussion of sexual difficulties. Ruth complains of the lack of eros in the relationship, and David defensively claims that it's just beginning to grow.

The secondary process includes all that is unintentional. For example, in the beginning Ruth's voice rose while announcing, 'I only said that I have been in a hole for a week.' David had experienced her comments about their sex life as a reproach and reacted defensively. She, in turn, spoke to his defensiveness by raising her voice aggressively. Since he is upset but wants to remain cool, she becomes aggressive. They are primarily talking about sex, but secondarily fighting about who is right or wrong. The secondary signals are fighting signals, not communications about sex.

Their double signals also appear in the way they are sitting. The therapist is on the chair, the husband is on the floor, and the wife is on the chair above her husband. She sits higher up than he in a more dominant and extraverted position. His sitting position is a sign of his defensiveness. The therapist could have chosen to work with these positions by switching them around at the beginning.

SYMMETRICAL REACTIONS

When Ruth complained that she needed more from David and the therapist encouraged her to reach out directly to him, she responded that she could not because he would not do the same. This is a typical symmetrical reaction: 'If you do not change, then I will not change, if you cannot, then I cannot!!' Symmetrical behavior is not simply a power entanglement which keeps people from growing, but is due to a shared dream and edge. Both are unable to reach out and be direct. Hence, to begin with, they need encouragement to be consciously indirect, and to realize the trouble they have in being direct.

SYMPTOMS AS DOUBLE SIGNALS

When David is attacked for not being erotic, he coughs. He

says that he is not well. He asks that she let him get rid of his cold before he approaches her sexually. It seems as if his cough is somatized defensiveness. Symptoms arise or coincide with a situation in which an individual is not strong or aware enough to consciously support a particular signal, in this case needing time to gain strength to defend himself.

THIRD PARTY POLITICS

Though Ruth admitted that she could not animate her husband, she continues to try by using a form of blackmail, a threat pattern which I call 'third party politics.' She warns him that she will find another lover to meet her needs if David does not. Third party politics happens all the time. Whenever a party feels too weak to get its point across to a second party, it brings in an absent third party, a party which supports it in some way. The power of this tactic lies in the fact that the second party cannot defend itself against the third one since the third is not really present. If we look at Ruth closely, however, we find her lover in a double signal, in her production of erotic fantasies which attempt (inadequately) to care for her.

CLOWNING

When the therapist asks David to help Ruth with her bubble bath, he clowns. He makes jokes instead of telling Ruth to stop threatening him. His clowning maintains the primary process of discussing absent topics and avoiding expressions and feelings. Such clowning is important; it indicates an attempt to cover up hurt and fear. The therapist could have simply said to the clown, 'Clown around until you discover what feelings you can disguise by joking.'

THE QUESTION

When Ruth realizes that the third party threat is not helping, she turns to David and asks him what he's thinking. But this question is a trap; it can never be satisfactorily answered since she really wants to make a statement like, 'You ass, be nice to me!' David responds to the question by saying that he is troubled by coughing and drinking. Why is he asking for time? Ruth ignores his reply and comments that she needs more love. She doesn't hear his answer because she wasn't interested in her own question! Be careful, most questions are primary processes which hide statements!

DREAMS
We could easily guess what this couple is dreaming knowing that double signals are dreambody manifestations. David dreamed that a young man was angry about doing social work and was repairing a machine that could be used as a weapon, and Ruth dreamed about a man she likes who is himself at home but falls apart in groups. David's dream shows that he is irritated by his sociability and preparing for war. Internally he is arming himself for a battle. Ruth's dream implies that she, too, does not yet have the strength to be genuine with others; it is easier for her to be 'at home,' that is, to fantasize about life.

AMPLIFYING THE TOTAL PROCESS
To amplify the total process, I would recommend to David that he behave as sweetly as possible. He should be polite, stay on the floor, and ask his wife to boss him around, telling her that he's a defenseless man, not yet ready to interact directly. Whenever she provokes him, he should tell her that he prefers coughing to defending himself. I would tell Ruth to demand that he be responsive and wake up but to tell him that she herself doesn't have the strength to do what she wants others to do.

WORKING WITH EDGES
Asking this couple to jump over their edges and be direct would probably not work. Pushing takes a lot of energy and doesn't hold. I prefer to paint the picture the way it is now and depend upon the intelligence of the collective dreambody itself and reorganize its parts. The creative potential of the individual will then awaken and make readjustments. This couple obviously needs to be more direct and conscious, but they cannot do so without

realizing how and where they are indirect and unconscious.

If people go over their edges too quickly, they either hurt each other physically or cannot benefit from what happened. Frequently they are simply not able to carry out the new behavior because it lies too far over the border of the edge. Direct interaction requires behavior patterns this couple does not yet have. The development of these new patterns is implied in their dreams and double signals but is not yet conscious. In David's case, he first has to repair his weapons before he can defend himself. Ruth has to learn what it means to be herself in public. Developing new internal patterns is a task which occurs most rapidly when old patterns are first brought to awareness and consciously lived.

DON AND PAULA

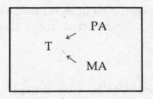

A young married couple walked into my room, sat quietly on the sofa and floor, and looked straight ahead at me and sideways at each other. They said they had come to the end of the road together, they simply could not get along anymore. Paula said she couldn't develop together with Don because he wouldn't allow her to be herself. She said she had dreamed that she was violent with him on a street car in Zürich and then affectionate afterwards. He said that he dreamed he was scared of falling off a chair.

After hearing their stories, I recommended that they speak directly to one another. Paula immediately stood up and approached him, pushing him backwards with anger. He said he wanted to stop the work because he was afraid of what he would do to her. As he spoke, she moved back against the wall, looked down, and became depressed.

```
┌─────────────────────────────┐
│                             │
│                   PA        │
│                             │
│   T                         │
│                             │
│                   MA        │
│                             │
└─────────────────────────────┘
```

As they were both visually oriented, I imitated them and told them to watch and tell me what they saw. As I played her, Paula said, looking at me, that if she really believed what she was saying, she would just let go and fight with him. He said he wanted to respect his fears. I sat down and they both began to physically fight with each other. The fight soon turned into a dance, a form of archaic, kinesthetic communication. They fought and laughed, she bit and screamed while he struggled and wrestled with her in a very friendly, ape-like way. A few minutes later they were both lying on my floor, exhausted and satisfied with what happened.

ANALYSIS
Paula said she needed to be violent with him but had been afraid to because she thought women were supposed to be delicate, feeling, and motherly towards their husbands. I told her that public opinions must be changing, even within her, otherwise she wouldn't dream of fighting with him on the street cars in Zürich!

In the Paula and Don unit, he is that part of her which has been too shy to express itself in public, and she is the part of him pulling him to the floor. Both have an edge against aggression. She believed a woman should not be aggressive, and he believed that if he was really aggressive, he would lose control of himself and kill her or hurt himself.

AGGRRESSION
When I played their roles, I gave them a chance to see how they looked in their relationship. They had been unnecessarily verbal with each other. Together, they are a dreambody

whose parts are trying to be more primitive and kinesthetic. They represent two different parts of the same dream: one part wants aggression and the other part represses it. As a body with two parts, one is violent partly because the other is physically shy. She dreams him up because she is afraid of herself, and he dreams her up to be violent because of his own hesitations.

THEIR MYTH
When I asked them about their early dreams, only Paula could remember one. In the beginning of their relationship, she dreamed that her grandmother who had died long ago was back in life. Her association to her grandmother was that she had been the wildest one in the family and consequently the one her mother liked the least. From this dream, we can guess that one of the governing patterns behind this couple is the return of an archaic, female principle. For Paula, this meant being her physical self in relationships. Don said that for him it meant not having to be unnecessarily sweet and well-behaved with Paula or with anyone else. He added that he had originally chosen Paula for her primitivity *and* lady-like behavior. Paula interrupted him at this point and insisted that she liked both her primitive and lady-like sides, but the latter could come into being only when the former was allowed to live first.

The background problem bothering Don and Paula is that strong kinesthetic communication outside of sex is forbidden in our culture. People touch each other either sexually or violently. Animal play and non-verbal expression in relationships is usually repressed.

Another interesting part of their work is the fact that getting over their edge and fighting resulted in playing. Why is that? People believe that if they go over their edges they will go crazy, be deserted, or become violent. But if their dreams pattern behavior on the other side of the edge, when they go over their edges, the wisdom of the flow, the Tao itself, takes over and relating in the deepest sense begins. When people no longer have control over themselves or their relationship, the world does *not* stop, in fact, it begins anew. It creates itself, reorganizing in an unimaginable way. This self-organizing principle of the universal dreambody lies behind my trust and belief in process: it is characteristic of the deepest experiences people can have together.

CHANNELS OF THE TIME

Paula's dream governed their relationship for years to come. Paula said that her grandmother had separated from her family in order to 'do her own thing.' Paula, too, sometime after the work we did together, left Don after a wild fight and then remarried him, just as in her dream she loved him after fighting with him. Here we see how the myth governs not only the momentary situation, but the whole relationship process.

Since her first dream happened on the streets of Zürich, and her grandmother was an unusual woman for the times, I must also ask myself how closely this couple's process is connected to the problems of our times. My guess is that the personal psychology of this couple is also a picture of our period in history, of the collective situation of European women in the 1980s.

Chapter 9
TYPICAL RELATIONSHIP PROCESSES

CHEMISTRY AND TYPOLOGY

When studying typology it is useful to see people as an alchemist would. Alchemists worked with chemical elements which gathered together and formed compounds through meshing. People gather together and through fighting, loving, and hating combine to form compounds. Think of the typical older couple. The logical, thinking-type man has split-off, unintegrated feelings. Because his feelings are free floating, he dreams his wife up to act them out. In this typical couple, the woman takes over the household and the man earns the money. She does his earthly, eros tasks for him and he loves her for this. Meanwhile, he is dreamed up by her to be logical and rational, which are exactly the elements missing from her consciousness. Together they form a completed, functioning unit.

He fulfills her archaic needs and vice versa. Thus, in the beginning of their relationship, they may experience heaven on earth. Like the celestial marriage of sun and moon, they are fascinated by each other and bound together by their mutual completion. During this phase, they feel like mirror images of each other, and even begin to look alike. They unconsciously integrate each other. He may begin to act more feeling while she acts more rationally.

THE PROCESS OF LOOKING LIKE YOUR PARTNER

Later in life, they may even assume the same body gestures,

postures, and peculiarities. How does this unconscious integration of the partner happen? It usually happens without effort or control. As you will remember from earlier chapters, the husband projects an inner image consisting of his own gestures and double signals on to his wife. She does the same. In the course of time, he slowly identifies with the gestures he projects on to her and starts to take on her facial and physical expressions. The same process occurs with her so that they begin to resemble each other. This comes about through unconscious identification with double signals and the integration of dream figures. You see this change happen quickly and radically (albeit temporarily) in body work when an individual feels and then moves like the dreambody experience within him.

HOW RELATIONSHIPS BEGIN
Typology explains a lot about how and why two people come together. It tells us that they feel completed through the experience of the other person who carries something which is secondary to them. However, typology does not explain everything. It predicts that any two opposite types would come together, and, as we know, this is not always the case.

There must be thousands of connections which illuminate the mysterious experience of love and relationship. One is typology and, as we have seen in previous chapters, another is a common dream. Remember for example the young couple from the last chapter, Paula and Don? They may hate each other, they may fight and try to beat each other up, they may part and come together but the factor which holds them together through this immense journey is a shared dream, a myth which is symbolized in the dream of fighting and loving on the Zürich tram or by the dream of the unusual grandmother. As long as this couple is together they share these dreams, they are coupled through the metaphor of the wild and unusual feminine element. In ordinary language this means that they share unusual and unconventional ways of relating. Whatever Don might do, whether he is a scientist or artist, whether Paula becomes an accountant, psychologist, or housewife, regardless of what becomes of them, they are together as long as they share this unconventional feeling attitude. She may want to leave him because he hurts her feelings, and he may get fed up with her because she is so uncoventional, but when they are parted, she will continue to be unconventional, and he will continue to deal with others in an unusual feeling manner. Thus, even if they do not like it, they are still coupled.

COLLECTIVE CONNECTIONS

It seems that couples, families, and groups have a dream or myth behind them, a saga searching for people to populate it. The myth dreams up the people to come together. The local myth is connected to the immediate environment in which the people live. It belongs to the city, nation, state, world, and universe. In fact, the kinds of myths and dreams which bind people together are aspects of the time, place, and universe in which they live.

THE LONELY HERO

Another way of describing this aspect of relationships is that there is almost always a creative, unlived, unusual, and mythical part in each individual which the individual finds difficult to support and which finds understanding, recognition, and appreciation in the new partner. Typical parts finding recognition are the heroic male, the artist, the passionate or powerful female, the sensitive boy, the dreamy girl, the chivalrous male, the mediumistic female, etc.

This powerful bonding in the beginning of the relationship creates unconsciousness so that the figure in each individual obtains support to surface against the rest of the personality which normally cannot support it.

Troubles begin when the individuals involved begin to integrate these parts themselves. At this moment they have less need for the other partner and they begin to grow out of the myth which has held them together. This is the point where the discussion of the early dreams and events in relationship can be very useful.

Remember the couple mentioned on page 72. His memory was that they didn't make love when they first met. Her first dream was that he shot her in the vagina. His sensitivity and need for freedom from performing in bed was nourished by the beginning of that relationship, and her need to contain what she called her promiscuous sexuality was supported. But as he grew, he no longer needed that protection and she no longer needed to be a nun; their relationship crisis and need for separation mirrored their growing out of the old pattern. They had lived through part of their lives which no longer existed and were in need of and ready for a change.

FACTORS IN SEPARATION

Thus, integration of unconscious aspects of the personality and growing through early patterns strains a relationship. But there are other psychic changes which also manifest themselves as relationship problems. An entire culture may be in the midst of change, and the dream dreaming up a given couple may begin to change in accordance with the changing times. Such changes create and destroy relationships. I have frequently seen how homosexual relationships occur after heterosexual ones in accordance with an emerging myth of our modern world that people must learn to love, wherever and however it appears, merging individuals who otherwise would be separated by religion, color, class distinction, and sexual preferences.

AN EXAMPLE

This reminds me of a couple which demonstrated the myth structuring a family system. They came from a Third World country where they enjoyed an immense and extended family life encompassing several hundred people and many generations. Each time this couple came to see me they complained about one another and said they wanted to work on their relationship but sat at opposite ends of my practice. One day, after amplifying his sitting position, he said, 'You know, we do not belong together.'

'Tell her why,' I said.

'I do not know' he said, 'I just do not know, it is like a bad dream.'

'What do you dream?' I countered.

Whereupon he said, 'I do not believe in dreams.'

'Tell me just a little one,' I said, 'one you do not believe in.'

'I dreamed recently that the world has changed,' he answered, 'that all the fairy tales which have been are no longer valid.'

I thought to myself, this is the dream of a new world, but what will this mean in their relationship? We worked together, first as a threesome, then together with some of their children, and once with their entire family of origin. It turned out that this family should not try to understand this man. Her family sided with her in rejecting his ideas about needing to live in a western country. He wanted to stay in their land, but finally decided to leave his family system and country and move to the 'new world.'

This was simultaneously a relief and tragic parting for all. It is the kind of process which must have occurred frequently during the colonization of America. It is an archetypal parting in which one member is called upon to change. He must then take the blame or credit for creating a chain effect or disturbance in the tradition of which he is a part. He is the dream of the community.

DEALING WITH THE OUTER FORMS OF RELATIONSHIP

How a couple integrates their relationship in a given culture is an utterly individual matter. Some couples need to keep their relationship a secret; others integrate it directly into their culture. Homosexual couples in certain cities must now stand up for their relationship; it is necessary not only for them but for the world around them. Others must get married or live together in a household. Ending relationships and separating is more fashionable and more of an option today in the western world than it has ever been.

RUNNING AWAY FROM RELATIONSHIP

Many separations and divorces are due to the individual's

inability to process the strains occurring from the individuation processes of one or both of the members, not
from incompatibility. When a separation occurs for this
reason, the same problems will be recreated in the next
relationship with another partner. The same problems arise
again, creating a cycling effect of dropping and beginning
relationships. Such cycling coincides with depression and
hopelessness.

There are also many couples, however, which should be
parting and which cannot for one reason or another. In
these cases terminal illnesses arise (particularly in the latter
part of life) and are often experienced as a chance to leave an
imprisoning relationship. Trying to live a myth which does
not belong to the individual creates violent psychosomatic
reactions. Periods of *individual* individuation, typological
change, transformation, external economic changes, death,
marriage, and birth in a family produce the greatest stress
on the family dreambody as it begins to dissolve, separate,
and recreate itself. Without the tools of communication
theory, dream work, and family therapy many couples
suffer through these periods in the most isolated and painful
ways. Some become permanently estranged without ever
having realized that the changes responsible for the stress
were only temporary phases of individuation. Of course
there are other couples who seem to be born with a sense of
fairness and good will and manage by luck and sheer
ruggedness to live through crisis periods.

Since each couple, family, and group is different, there are
no typical periods in a group's development. But certain
phases are outstanding from a psychotherapeutic viewpoint
and may be worth discussing. I want to stress, however,
that the phases which follow are not stages which people
'should' go through.

HEAVEN ON EARTH
The experience of heaven on earth may occur spontaneously
and miraculously in the beginning of relationships. Powerful
attractions arise by either consciously or unconsciously
integrating the other. This period is experienced as a

breakthrough; each member feels complete internally and externally. Double signals disappear, and there seem to be no edges blocking relationship and communication. Secondary processes become primary and the ensuing high is usually accompanied by a justifiable fear that the harmonious structure will not last long.

CULTURE

This phase of the relationship process usually consists of role assignments. Each partner identifies with a main typology and edges are formed to prevent role switching and continue the homeostatic functioning of the partnership, family, group, or society. As all partners fulfill their roles and functions, aggression, negativity, and unhappiness drop from awareness and reappear in dream figures and double signals. The edges become firm laws which may be implicitly or explicitly formulated, as in the case of a marriage contract. Our culture's marriage laws correspond to the ancient belief systems of Judeo-Christian theology and Roman law.

BOREDOM AND IRRITATION

Edges and the associated laws create homeostasis, the attempt to maintain harmony. During this stage of a couple's evolution, the drive for freedom and individuation resist the role-oriented primary process. It's usually in this phase that the family is planned. While the laws and edges are primarily respected, the double signals of individuation begin to surface. At this point the glow of harmony begins to wear off and partners recognize annoying and irritating characteristics in each other. They typically attribute this to the confines of married life and say that 'the honeymoon is over.'

CRISIS

Little irritations come and go, and in time produce a crisis; one partner's need to be an individual attacks the primary idea of peace and harmony. The other partner responds with rage against the threatening dissolution. But since the first partner's drive for freedom is still relatively unconscious and appears only in double signals, he cannot understand the other's rage. Because neither can fully identify with the secondary processes they are double signalling, they cannot accept the accusations levelled at them. Thus, they next accuse each other of lying. A communication crisis arises; one side no longer trusts the other. If mutual mistrust prevails, the crisis is usually dealt with by splitting up and abandoning communication altogether. Couples who cannot bear the tension of the battle switch or drop partners in the false belief that being alone or finding another partner will recreate the permanent state of harmony which was promised and protected by the preceding laws.

WORKING WITH CRISES

A governing paradigm of process work is that the process which presents itself in the moment contains all the elements necessary for its own solution.

If the therapist works with just one member of the couple, that member's disturbing double signals will disappear. In cases where the other partner refuses to come into therapy, it seems to be the first partner's fate to develop alone and learn how to adapt to the other's process. Some couples insist upon coming together. With the therapist's help the couple can learn to use the attacks and accusations as a challenge to further development. The attacks challenge them to come closer to their feelings and to stand up more strongly for their individual needs. Although both members want to win a battle, no one wins a war between secondary processes. The apparently weaker element always finds indirect and powerful methods which destroy the apparently stronger element. In most cases, processing the relationship results in more powerful and awakened people and a more differentiated couple.

A couple which has been together gets reborn when the cycle of blaming and denying comes to an end. Either this period ends by itself or one member admits to the other's accusations and tries to change. In situations where the accusation is of unpredictability, freedom, or independence the accuser must eventually face the end of dependency, while the accused has to stand up for the consequences of the process he initiated.

An interesting paradox lies at the center of this phase of development: the same process separating the couple may connect it as well. Most couples act decently, yet are simultaneously consumed by the drive for greater freedom. Getting beyond the edge of decency allows both to interact and contact levels of experience and freedom previously only dreamed of. The identification with the role of the victim or persecutor then switches, creating a strong sense of relationship which was only vaguely implicit in the earlier accusations.

THE DOUBLE EDGE FACTOR

Regardless of their goals, couples and small groups find that in a relationship crisis, the greatest relief occurs when each individual involved has gone over an edge. If two people are involved in a crisis, the factor determining whether or not the relationship experience will be satisfactory is the double edge factor.

An example of the double edge is a couple who came to see me because the husband wanted help for his wife who had been hospitalized two years earlier because of a psychotic episode. This couple has been in a steady, unending conflict for years. As they came in she murmured in a drugged state, 'I'm sick.' I immediately said, 'I believe that, but only in part. Your illness must in some way be a reaction to what is happening in the world around you.' She countered, 'I have never been unhappy with my husband.' I said, 'Not even the last time you were unhappy?' Then a story slipped out in which she got angry at him because he stayed out late, drinking with some of his friends.

She said, 'He is a good man . . . oh . . . oh . . . here it comes . . . I see the nuclear catastrophe on the moon.' I said, 'Let's all go to the crazy moon, and make a nuclear explosion about his drinking. Now!' Whereupon she yelled at him in the most sober, undrugged fashion, 'You were mean to me.' He was naturally not the least bit happy about her now normal behavior and yelled back, 'Stop being so emotional,' and then he yelled at me, 'You supported her, but not me.' I then sat behind him to support him and held him while he cried like a child, begging for help. Later he told me that this was the first time he had ever cried as an adult.

There were two edges in this work; there was hers, the edge to being aggressive and his, the edge to showing his emotions. Both needed support to get through the crisis created by their own necessary growth. Going over only one edge creates an imbalance in the homeostatic functioning of a couple or family and throws the group into great turmoil because the individual who has not gotten sufficient support to go over his edge resents the therapist.

Whenever possible, either both edges should be crossed or none at all. If only one edge is crossed, then the couple should be warned about the potential irritation of the partner who has not gone over an edge. He will complain about injustice or frustration after the session. The same happens in individual work if only one part of the personality is supported, i.e. only a dream or secondary process. In this situation, the individual should be warned that his primary process, which was not fully appreciated during the sitting, will soon have a big reaction.

INDIVIDUALITY OF RELATIONSHIPS

The result of processing relationships is that couples become individual. It is virtually impossible to understand them from the outside because what one expects two people to feel and do is rarely what they are actually doing. Programs such as support, mutual love and understanding, free expression, individuality, etc., are usually not the patterns which tie people together. Some of the momentary individual processes of couples may be: mother one another, mother the son, doctor the patient, repress feeling, hide sexuality, do not communicate, become shamans, etc.

THE TAO OF RELATIONSHIPS

The faltering laws of our society governing relationships

indicate the necessity for a new form of relationships. What will this new form of relationship look like? Process concepts imply a new paradigm for relationships. The process worker not only forwards the rules and regulations of the primary process, but is also trained to be aware of the subtle and extensive dreambody language of love, friendship, and growth. There are already many couples and families who have developed the necessary awareness to relativize cultural rules and regulations with moment to moment awareness of communication signals. These people may be the first Taoists: those learning how to let process organize the evolution of love and friendship. An apparent paradox lies at the bottom of love; having deep and growing relationships depends upon courage and disciplined signal awareness.

In a relationship crisis, this means that instead of holding on to your position and defending your opinion, you become aware of your process and that of your partner. If the Tao sends the message of softness, let go and be soft. Instead of acting like a rational computer when you are unhappy or jealous, be unhappy, follow your jealousy. Instead of being proud when you are hurt, pursue your hurt and pain. Instead of acting like an adult when you are really a cry baby, cry like a baby. Instead of being democratic when you have a personal need, try to wear the clothes of a dictator, but do it consciously. If you feel loving in the midst of a fight, then be affectionate. If you are depressed, sink to the bottom of the earth. If you are hopeless, express your fears about never being loved. One thing then changes to another, making relationships an indescribably, simultaneous initiation of two or more people into the essence of life.

Chapter 10
THE UNIVERSAL DREAMBODY

In ancient beliefs relationships were made in heaven, organized by the gods, and determined by the constellation of stars at the moment of birth. Depending upon the period and location in history, they are governed by fate, karma, or the Tao. In modern theory they are organized by culture, love, or complexes. In modern psychology, the individual marries the father, the mother, or the unrealized self. In this chapter I continue this search for underlying structures and factors in relationship by discussing field effects, dreambodies, holograms, and the myth of the world anthropos. The theory which will organize the facts surrounding relationships is the universal dreambody. It has field characteristics, behaves in any moment like a hologram, and evolves like an immense human being, or anthropos.

FIELD EFFECTS

Let's consider the empirical reality. I worked with a couple in a seminar house in the Swiss Alps. They came to the workshop to find more excitement in their marriage, which, after twenty-five years, they described as 'good, but insufficient.' This couple's myth was established by a memorable event in the beginning of their relationship; the car carrying them to the wedding burst into flames.

Their primary process was to love and nurture each other; their secondary process is fiery energy and excitement. Suddenly, in the midst of their session with me, a fire broke out in the kitchen of the chalet. One of the seminar participants had been baking an apple pie when all of a sudden the oven caught on fire. All of us were awe-struck by the connection between the fire in the kitchen and the inner fire, the energy this couple was seeking. A hard-nosed observer could cut off the emotional element involved in the synchronicity and simply call it 'luck' or 'chance.' A more useful way to view such a synchronicity would be to see it as the secondary process which has been split off from the couple and which, therefore, appears in dreams, double signals, and even the surrounding world.

This view sees the environment as part of the couple's dreambody and, conversely, sees the couple as a part of the larger body of the world. This field view has a great deal of explanatory power for the process of the entire group at the moment of the fire. The group process at that seminar had been, until the fire, cooking apple pies for each other and filtering out the fiery affects and conflicts which broke out later in battles between the participants.

Thus, a couple can be a channel for a group, and, likewise, the group or environment can be a channel for the couple. The dynamics of this operate like a hologram; that's why I also refer to this as a hologram theory. Imagine the hologram as a piece of glass with a detailed picture on it. If you drop it on the floor and break it into hundreds of pieces, each little piece will contain the exact pattern that existed on the larger original. The world we live in behaves, in many respects, like a hologram. It's broken up into little segments: nations, cities, religions, groups, or families, and each of these smaller segments carries the same pattern found in the world as a whole.

DREAMING UP, PROJECTION, AND HOLOGRAM THEORY

The phenomena of dreaming up and projection fit into hologram theory. As we have seen in previous chapters, one person can 'carry' a dream which refers to his personal process. Yet, when he nears another person, this individual dream suddenly takes on collective characteristics; it organizes the projections and the body movements of everyone involved. If you dream of a conflict between yourself and another dream figure or between two dream figures, there is almost a one hundred percent chance that you will become involved in a relationship conflict on that day.

OCCUPATION OF HOLOGRAM

I have pointed out in *Working with the Dreaming Body* that the occupation of the couple's dreambody or hologram depends upon availability. For example, a woman with a strong negative father experience dreams that she is the victim of her father's brutality. When she is around her husband who is tougher and less sensitive than she, the husband will become the tough father, while she will experience herself as the victim. This dream holds them together. Regardless of how much they dislike each other, she will be pressed to be with him to discover how to transform both the internal and external brutal father.

Chances are that this woman will have other friendships, and among them she will choose a woman who is much weaker than she is. The dream she carries with her will organize her friendship with the weaker woman. But now, since she is tougher than her friend, our dreamer will experience herself as the father in this couple, and it is possible that her friend will sometimes feel like a victim!

Consider a man who has learned to please people and dreams that he is under the domination of his mother, whom he otherwise loves. He is a bit of a mother's boy insofar as he has a tendency to fulfill other people's expectations. This dream works in his environment as well. If he marries a woman who is more forceful and definitive than he is, then she will become the evil, dominating mother (at least in his mind) while he will experience himself as having to obey and fulfill her expectations.

He carries this hologram with him wherever he goes; the occupation of the pattern depends upon who is present. Hence, if the other business people at the office are less requiring than he, he will become the dominant one and boss the others around. They in turn take on the weaker role and must obey. Thus, this man will believe he is henpecked only in the company of his wife. Naturally he will attribute this to 'her' domineering nature.

Therefore, the part of a person or group which is available and which best fits a certain figure in the hologram receives that role to play. Hence, the role you play in a given family depends upon who else is present; in another family you may be completely different. Since most people have the drive to experience all parts of themselves, you can now understand why people have the need to have many relationships, for they experience different parts of themselves in each relationship.

PARADIGM SHIFTS

In the early years of this century, psychology explained individual peculiarities in terms of individual behavior. People were viewed as single indivisible entities, like particles in classical physics. Accordingly, the world was understood as the sum of its individual parts. However, family studies, couple therapy, the existence of synchronicities, double signals, and psychosomatic phenomena indicate that the theory of the individual requires the complementary theories of the dreambody and hologram. These theories envision the behavior of the universe as a hologram: a universe patterned by collective dreams and which appears as a collective body composed of you, me, the stove in the kitchen, and the trees outside.

THE COLLECTIVE UNCONSCIOUS

Jung was chiefly responsible for introducing non-causal ideas into modern psychology. He called the field we live in the collective unconscious and claimed that this field was patterned by archetypes, much in the same way the stars in the sky are patterned by constellations and their associated myths, once thought to govern the behavior of the universe.

According to Jung's theory, archetypes are 'forms without content, representing merely the possibility of a certain type of perception or action.' Those readers who are familiar with the I Ching will know that the idea of the archetypes is not new. It is found not only in modern physics and psychology, but in Taoism as well. There, a governing 'Tao' is a field with lines of force or 'dragon lines.' These dragon lines organize such diverse events as the volcanic eruption of a nearby mountain, the President's stomach ache, a crisis in the Middle East, and the flip of the coins when you consult the *I Ching*.

ANTHROPOS THEORY

Hologram theory goes back centuries, way before Jung and even the Taoists. Holograms were imagined to be gods who governed the universe. They were gigantic, human-like figures which mythologists call anthropos images. The Buddhists, for example, believed in a great and wise Being called the Atman, in whom we all live. The goal of life in many eastern religions is to become one with this Being. Jews and Christians believe that man was created in God's image. Many religions consider the universe to be a gigantic, human-like god who, when divided into pieces, becomes the different elements of the world. His hair becomes the trees, his breath becomes the wind, his blood becomes the rivers, etc. In her book, *Creation Myths*, von Franz describes how the anthropos figure was believed to be simultaneously the world and its creator. Some myths indicate that upon awakening the anthropos creates the world. Others believe that he 'dreams' the world into existence. In many myths, when he is killed or dies, he goes to pieces. The world, its wind, sun, stars, and waters are created from his individual body parts.

His periodic awakening, sleep, and death are mythical explanations for the eternal experience of history and for our perception of the division and unity of our planet. As long as the anthropos is awake and well, harmony and order prevail. But when he dies or falls ill, the mysterious experience of unity falls asunder and we find ourselves lonely, isolated individuals in the midst of a large and frightening universe. At this moment, we are like the hologram shattered into a million pieces. Each one of us is a tiny fragment containing the image of the whole, struggling as best we can to put ourselves back together.

When the anthropos goes to pieces, our social structures and institutions totter and become shaky. The world is threatened by catastrophies, our religions falter, and family systems are plagued by crises. In the last chapter we saw how a family or group is strained by the individuation process of one member who may grow, die, form a friendship outside the group, have children, or fall seriously ill. All of these changes batter the entire family system, and the homeostatic organism, like the crumbling anthropos, topples as change crashes up against rigidity. Here we must consider the possibility that the individuation process of the individual is actually a function of the overall process of the dreambody or anthropos: no one person can be held absolutely responsible even for his personal behavior!

CREATION AND ANNIHILATION

The process of creation and destruction of the anthropos is patterned after the periodic struggles of the individual; he spirals through existence, conflicts within himself, goes to 'pieces,' and comes together again, either in this life or in another world.

The evolution of the anthropos is similar. We fear that our world will go to pieces and wonder if it will ever come together. Couples and groups come together, separate, and recreate themselves. The difference between the evolution of a couple, family, and group and the evolution of an individual is that the evolution of an individual is more rapid than that of a large group, nation, or planet. It is frequently possible to reach some sort of satisfactory solution to a conflict between the parts of an individual within an hour. In family work three or four sessions are usually required to reach the same state. There is a big difference between the individual and his parts and the couple or group and its parts. While the individual may fear death, it rarely stops him from examining his parts and attempting to put them together. A couple, however, is in a more precarious position; the partners are never sure that the relationship will hold up and stand the strain of growth and development. Mythology tells us that when the anthropos dies, his parts fly asunder and relate to each other in a new way. Thus, when groups and families divide, the individuals relate to one another in new ways. Before, they were parts of a family; now they are parts of the world. Could it be that so many separations happen today because we are meant to experience ourselves as part of a world as well as parts of a family?

THE GLOBAL DREAMBODY

I have been using several ideas from psychology, mythology, physics, and dreambody theory to understand the global dreambody which organizes relationships. Let's assemble the characteristics of this dreambody and demonstrate its relationship to other theories and systems. Note that:

In the global dreambody
1 The whole is patterned.
2 Each part contains the whole.
3 Each part is related to all other parts causally and non-causally.
4 The whole creates and heals itself.
5 The whole can destroy or make itself ill.
6 The whole has mythical characteristics.
7 The whole has a flip-flop occupation rule.
8 The whole has a human character.
9 The whole is the goal of human development.

The global dreambody, including field, hologram, dreambody and anthropos theories, helps organize what we see, feel, and hear from individuals, groups, couples, and families. The aspects of relationships which are difficult to understand within individual or family-centered paradigms can be organized under the concept of the global dreambody. It is an anthropos figure with a process, a life and death of its own, like the rest of us. The anthropos' myth of creation and annihilation, of becoming human and dreaming himself into being, reveals how couples divorce and assemble, struggling with growth like an individual.

The coagulation and separation of an individual's parts is the essence of awareness and consciousness. Thus, the anthropos also grows in awareness of himself through periods of strife and union. Just as we find out more about our belly if we have a belly ache, so he finds out more about us when we have trouble and finds out how we relate to the rest of the world we live in. His growing self-awareness is reflected in our growing awareness of the community and universe in which we live. His increased awareness is reflected in our burgeoning interest in psychology!

The global dreambody operates like an individual dreambody by organizing the patterns, dreams, and fantasies of the individual parts. People move, get sick and dream in correlation with their organizing myths. Double signals, incongruent and congruent behavior, and primary and secondary processes are causal and mechanical aspects of communication between the parts of the universal dreambody and indicate its field-like operation. Yet at the same time, and from a larger viewpoint, the global dreambody is a non-causal field with synchronistic connections which are organized by patterns without any known, outside mechanical influence on the parts. In addition, the global dreambody operates like a hologram insofar as its individual parts reflect the same patterns as all the other parts and of the whole.

PROCESSING CHANGE

Whether transformations in the universal dreambody lead to world war or peace is not merely up to God but up to all of us involved. At present there are two central problems in the way we work with change. The first is our knowledge and attitude towards the different parts of ourselves. We believe in democracy only outside of ourself. Inside, all the childish parts, the rage, jealousy, sexiness, egotism, and ambition suffer discrimination. They are condemned and repressed; but any part locked away will only strike out later against the ruling order. Any 'evil' pressed out of the primary process will eventually overwhelm and surprise us and contribute to disturbing relationships. If we are not open to all our parts, we will not be able to change them, instead, they will change us! The result is that we will be possessed by them, like a country dominated by a formerly repressed tyrant; this is what inevitably leads to world war.

Being childish, emotional, jealous, and hurt all belong, or *should* belong, to our self-image.

The second outstanding problem in the way we process change can be seen as both a religious and scientific problem. It's a problem of belief, and of how we view the world and feel about it. This problem is what I call the therapist's attitude.

Chapter 11
THE THERAPIST'S ATTITUDE

Knowledge of the dreams, fields, and anthropos organizing individual and collective life has certain implications for the therapist as well as the client; it has the potential to change the therapist's attitude towards himself and his clients.

THE WHOLE AND THE PARTS

When I work with one person, I don't just see each individual dream figure and body symptom, but the implications these have for the entire personality. Likewise, when I work with a couple or family, perceiving the collective field enables me to work with the troubled individual as a symptom, a tool used by the field to express itself. According to the theory, I cannot completely identify an individual with his role in a family, for I know that in another group of people he will play another part, perhaps even an opposite role to the one he plays now. This explains why most people have different kinds of friends. Though each friendship creates a dreambody field which could resemble other fields, the way the parts are populated in each field differs. A feeling type in one field may be pressed to be the thinking type in another!

SIDING WITH THE PROCESS

The dreambody field is constantly changing and constantly troubling primary processes which have become rigid. When working with an individual, the therapist who focuses upon process and not upon a solution sides with evolution. If I focus upon the changes a person goes through, then I avoid the behaviorist tendency to recommend that he change and develop new personality traits or behavioral patterns. By siding with change, I side with awareness of what is happening in any given moment and thereby avoid programming the person to be whole and balanced. On the other hand, I must be flexible enough to realize that a given behavior program might be just the process some people need!

Likewise, when working with a couple, I side with what they ask for as well as what is happening to them. By siding with their total process, I do not side unconditionally with any one of their dreambody's members, nor do I identify the individual with the dream figure of that particular moment.

ONE-SIDEDNESS

Despite the therapist's good intentions to stay as neutral as possible, he frequently finds himself in the difficult and unwelcome position of siding with one member of a couple or family. One member tells his story and the therapist sympathizes with him and wants to support him, believing him to be wronged by the others and in need of help. But then the picture changes when another member tells *his* side of the story, and the therapist finds his biases changing.

Under these circumstances, it would be ridiculous for the therapist to profess absolute objectivity and neutrality. Though, in principle, the fairest thing to do would be to declare neutrality, it would come immediately under the suspicion of the other members of the family. In fact, they would have every right to be suspicious, knowing that human nature is such that the therapist must have at least momentarily, specific preferences. If the therapist, however, sides permanently and unconditionally with one member, the family or group can be split up and severely harmed. This problem is especially acute when the therapist has been working more intensely with one member than with the others.

How can a therapist deal with his preferences? When the work begins and the couple begins to communicate, the therapist finds his allegiances constantly shifting from one to the other, regardless of whom he knows best. There are a few reasons for this. The first is that frequently the accusations flying back and forth between members may actually contain a kernel of truth. The therapist, in the disguise of a preference, is actually perceiving the truth behind an accusation. Though there may be a bit of truth in an accusation, it's virtually impossible for the accused to see and admit that the accusation is true. The most natural response in the world is to deny it and counter-accuse! The therapist could constructively use his preference of the moment by helping the members change one another. Accusations are not the most effective method of communication. When the therapist sees the truth in an accusation, the most helpful thing he can do is to try to make the accusation more acceptable to the accused by investigating the accuser's uncertainty. This will help strengthen the accuser.

The second reason a therapist has momentary preferences is that though one member is dissatisfied with another, he may not be able to express his dissatisfaction and, thus, unconsciusly forms a coalition with the therapist for more support for his feelings. The therapist, instead of being drawn into the coalition, can bring in his awareness and suggest that the coalition-maker might need support to say things he feels unable to say at home.

Siding frequently happens when the therapist is dreamed up by a member of a dreambody. He picks up the double signals, feelings, reactions, or opinions of one member who, at that time, cannot support or bring out those messages. Instead of becoming the voice of this member, the therapist can work with the person on his edge. He can encourage him to pick up that part and its messages and directly give him the support he's seeking through a coalition.

Sometimes the therapist has to wait a long time before he is able to act on his preferences. I remember once seeing a couple with their only child, a lonely, shy daughter. They were in the midst of a divorce. I immediately took sides with the daughter because of her introversion and fright when the parents began to fight. But every effort of mine to approach her only forced her further into a corner. The efforts her mother made to comfort her were also resisted. After a while I could no longer focus on the child but followed the adults' fight. They were fighting about who was going to have custody of the daughter after the divorce. Suddenly, in the midst of the battle arena, the little girl threw a little toy to us. I picked this up as a signal inviting me to play with her. She was playing 'family' with little dolls. In her game, the mother wanted to get rid of the daughter and make her stay with the father. So the daughter went to the father, but soon got sick. Then the mother had to come to the bedside, and the daughter told the mother that she needed her. At this moment, the real mother, watching the game, broke out into tears and admitted that she really had wanted to get rid of the girl because she thought the child no longer loved her. The mother felt guilty because she had taken the first step in breaking up the family by beginning an extramarital relationship. The daughter cried, too, and the father, of all things, smiled. Why? It turned out that the woman he was thinking of marrying already had too many children!

DREAMBODY WISDOM

If you take away the edges cutting off communication and follow the process, the parts connect and reorganize themselves spontaneously. How does this happen? This happens because each dreambody is an anthropos with its own primitive wisdom and intelligence. Repeated experiences indicate that if you help the body to awareness, it will do whatever necessary to reorganize itself creatively. If the therapist feels responsible for its well-being, then he has identified with the magical, creative power of dreams. Such an inflation leads directly to a depression about people and human nature. My suggestion is to take the humble job of making the unconscious conscious and let the mysterious thing called life do its own creating and reorganizing.

MEDDLING

It's of utmost importance not to meddle with nature. I remember a man who was married to an alcoholic woman who beat him, abused and insulted him in public, and fiercely hated him. He complained to me, and, naturally, I told him to fight back. But I did not trust myself, so I asked him to tell me a dream before he took my good advice. He told me that he frequently dreamed that he should be passive and not fight her! One day, after several weeks of his non-violence campaign, she accidentally burned the house down and killed herself in a drunken episode. He inherited a large sum of money which he never knew she had, soon remarried, and lived, more or less, happily ever after! The moral of this story is that no one, not even a well-trained and useful psychologist, knows the workings of fate. The therapist's task is not only to advise but to bring the unconscious to awareness and trust life to do the rest.

PERCEPTUAL CHANGES

Seeing a couple as a unit creates a perceptual change in the therapist's view of the world. If I look at a couple as a unit with connecting parts, I can expect an answer from any part when I pose a question to one member. This expectation opens up my perceptual system. In fact, when I work with a couple and ask one member a question, I frequently get the answer from another member, another channel, or even another object! Thus, in time, I find my eyes gazing at the space between people and seeing individuals as two points in a larger field. This new and unusual perceptual mode alters the therapist's view and disrupts his expectations of human behavior. Yet it enables him to open up his perception and awaken to the world around him.

AN EXAMPLE

Having a flexible focus allows the therapist to shift back and forth between individual and group. If he is inflexible, he creates boundaries around an individual and ignores the relationship problems occurring. On the other hand, if he creates the boundary around the family unit, he will miss the signals asking for individual attention and help.

I once worked with a family who came to see me because their child had developed a violent skin rash. The first time they came I noted that their primary process was to focus upon the family situation. They had read many books on modern psychology and felt that the whole family should come to work on the son's disease.

As soon as we began, the husband turned towards the window. I asked him if he wanted to leave, despite his intention to 'do family therapy.' He said he wanted to stay, but then confessed that he had been having an affair with a woman in another country that he visited periodically on business. The wife immediately declared that she could understand his behavior, and a minute later the little boy's devastating and unsightly rash broke out. I turned to the mother and worked on her edge against being emotional. She admitted that she was afraid to be jealous and confront her husband because he might leave her. Meanwhile, the child was becoming increasingly ill. The more the mother held her feelings back, the more disturbed the little boy became.

I decided to focus on her for the moment. The causal connection between jealousy, the edge against it, and the little boy's rash impressed me. At first I tried to use it and encouraged the mother to change. Finally, my focus ended up in a conflict with her. She argued that she was not emotional. I said she was. To reduce the tension surrounding the child, I begged the little boy to wait outside with his sisters. That did it. The mother exploded and accused me of breaking up the family. Realizing that this was their secondary process, I recommended that the father leave for a week, the kids stay with the grandmother, and the mother take off for a week on the Mediterranean with a friend. The family responded to my suggestion with anger. They left my office, acting harmonious and unified in their anger toward me. Two weeks later I saw them again and the father admitted that he really loved his wife and had only begun the affair to escape the stifling family atmosphere. The boy's rash had disappeared.

The point of this story is that my perceptual flexibility was limited at first. I wanted to see them only as a family unit and avoided interacting with the mother myself. I had made a program out of focusing on the family. But since this was just their problem, I changed my focus, paid attention to the mother, let the kids leave, and improved the overall situation.

DREAMBODY TENSION

Working with a family is at once easier and more difficult than working with an individual. It's easier because all parts are present and interacting. I can ask them directly what they are doing and feeling. I don't have to assume what the problems and edges are. The increased clarity in the collective dreambody is paid for by the equally increased tension. Sitting with the family or group full of edges and problems is like sitting near a bomb about to explode. No wonder its members often want to leave, the tension is acute and it takes immense courage to even enter the scene in the first place. I can easily understand why many therapists choose either not to work with families or else choose to organize family behavior into games dominated by clearly delineated rules and regulations.

THE MEANING OF FAMILY TENSION

The great tension and pain the therapist experiences in a family body is similar to the pain felt when individual body parts have trouble with one another, or like the pain God has experiencing all of us as parts of himself. There is no escaping this pain, either as a therapist or as a living, working member of a collective dreambody. The pain is relieved once the tension becomes so unbearable that the parts are forced over their edges and begin to communicate. I can only recommend that one take as much of the tension as possible and realize that it is also the tension and pain of the greater body which is at a loss as to how to work out these problems.

WORKING WITH TENSION

A sensitive therapist will realize that he functions as the family's medium. The sadness and stress he feels are a reaction to its pain. Thus, he can bring out those feelings verbally or discover them in the double signals and dreams of his clients. The fields around some families dream the therapist up to be rational, think things out, and make everything clear. Other families simply need a neutral party to be present. They don't want change, but encouragement and mothering. Some couples need only to be tolerated and appreciated.

DRAWING IN THE THERAPIST

The danger exists that the therapist will get unconsciously drawn into these fields and do for the family what it should be doing for itself. One of my students in a training session worked with a married couple. The wife was afraid of being jealous of another because she believed that jealousy was wrong. She needed strength to be jealous and stand up for it. She dragged her husband into the therapy session and then flirted with the therapist. The therapist felt complimented by her and after a while defended her by picking a fight with the husband. She was delighted, for it was just what she needed but could not do. The therapist had been unconsciously drawn into a coalition to support the wife.

I came into the training session in the midst of this messy situation and recommended that the woman play the therapist relative to her husband. I noted that she was afraid of her resistance to her husband and consequently set the therapist up to resist him for her. When she finally played the therapist and resisted the husband herself, she became much more interesting. The husband, surprisingly enough, did not get angry at her, but found her more dynamic and attractive!

Thus, the therapist as a medium means being a tool which the family's field can use to express itself. If he is aware of the part he contributes to the dreambody, he can actively use that role to benefit everyone. In an ideal situation, he notices what he feels, identifies it, and links it to the signals and process of one or all members of the family. If he is unaware of the role he is being asked to play in a family dreambody, he will never be able to give it back to the family system. As a result, the family will simply continue along, fully unconscious of their secondary process. The awareness and experience required to follow one's self, the outer situation, and the connections between the two is rarely, if ever, inherent in an individual. Therefore, I suggest to anyone interested in relationship work to enter analysis himself and ask for periodic supervision of process work, either 'live' or through video recordings.

SURPRISES

Consider the example of two children who were constantly fighting each other and who were brought to me by their parents. The boy was very shy. He turned and looked down at the floor every time his sister yelled at him. I worked with his posture and helped him to express verbally his need for quietness and his disinterest in fighting. As soon as he said it to her, they seemed to become the best of friends, and all four left my office happily.

How surprised I was the next day when the mother called me. She was concerned because the boy had locked himself in his room, and his sister had become deeply depressed. Had I been sufficiently aware of the overall process, I could have worked with it in my office. I should have helped the boy to turn away *physically* from his sister, not just verbalize his wish to her. I should have recognized that verbalizing was actually a form of contact he was not interested in. The next time I saw them, I corrected my mistake and encouraged the boy to turn his back on her, not just look down when she attacked him. Naturally, she became depressed and, with a little help, admitted that she needed, loved, and missed him. This confession touched the boy deeply. Both cried together and promised to respect each other's peculiarities. This scene was especially important for the parents because introversion was apparently forbidden and repressed in the family. When the sister decided to accept the boy's need for peace and quiet, the mother broke down and cried. She needed the same! The family decided to stop having so many obligatory family activities and to respect one another's need for privacy.

In this story, the boy carried the secondary process, the introversion, for the family. At first I missed the importance of his process, pressed him to sacrifice it for the sake of verbal communication with his sister, and thereby amplified its power. Thus, it broke out violently and surprisingly when he locked himself into his room. Everyone in the family, including the boy, was shocked; their primary process had been openness and togetherness.

If the therapist is caught by surprise by a partner or a client's action, he has missed a signal. He has ignored a secondary process and should educate himself in at least two ways. First, he must find out which signals he tends to miss, and second, he should discover why he misses and underestimates them. With greater awareness of signals and wiser evaluation of their implicit processes, it is highly unlikely that a client or partner will surprise the therapist. One should be able to see processes happening ahead of time. Physical illness, separation, marriage, divorce, psychosis, suicide, death, and pregnancy can all be spotted before they become visible.

WEAKNESS AND STRENGTH

In the long run, there is no weaker and no stronger member of a human unit. The weakest one, the baby, can get a rash which will turn the adult to desperation and bring him to his edge. I no longer feel badly for the typical 'henpecked' husband or the woman married to an insensitive, high-powered businessman. The apparently 'weaker' member of a pair has an inexhaustible range of secondary processes and 'magic spells' at his unconscious disposal which could crumble even the rock of Gibralter. The weaker one slowly chips away at the stronger one's lofty position by making him feel guilty for past wrongs, by subtle hints about the kids', neighbors', and friends' opinions about him, by ignoring him, by dropping double signals of hate and disgust, and in some cases even surprising him with a divorce summons.

The stronger member of a couple is never strong enough to show human feelings like hurt, jealousy, or fear, but instead, hypnotizes the weaker one by a computer-like persona when dealing with painful facts. The stronger one appears to win in the beginning because he represents the accepted primary process: coolness and nonchalance. Nevertheless, the apparently weaker one carries the all-powerful secondary process which will eventually determine the course of events.

I am convinced that even if the weaker one loses the initial fight, being a winner or loser is only an illusion. Moreover, one 'victory' in the game of life is immediately followed by the pain of receiving hurtful and revengeful double signals. Though novels and films portray happy endings to storybook romances, the process worker knows that beginnings and ends, winners and losers, and problems and solutions are only illusions of the primary process.

THE PHENOMENON OF AN UNSOLVABLE PROBLEM

What happens when a couple or family runs up against an unsolvable problem? If the therapist can't help them cross their edges and communicate with each other, they split into pieces. Each member goes to others outside the family to gossip, seek support, and ask for advice. Naturally, this can be judged negatively as a destructive and counter-productive process because it depletes the energy within the family by dispersing it into the environment. But it is more interesting to observe how seemingly unsolvable problems dissolve the family's boundaries, redefining the unit to include the larger, extended environment. Dropping the boundaries of one human unit and connecting to other units to form a greater anthropos can be seen as a function of unsolvable problems. The meaning of the problems can be understood when we consider that the anthropos, the larger unit, has a process which works itself out through its smaller parts. Thus, what can't be solved by the smaller units, serves as a piece of development for the larger anthropos. For example, an upper-class, white, surburban community will dream up one of its families to house thieves, gangsters, junkies, or murderers. Such a family may not be able to solve its problems internally because the greater community needs the family as a scapegoat, as a channel for the collective secondary processes. The hologram which includes this family is in the midst of developing a relationship to wildness, aggression, or other lost instincts. The total anthropos development contributes to the breakdown of family boundaries and the use of specific families for the greater good of the community.

Chapter 12
PLANETARY PSYCHOLOGY

Imagine that you are a therapist interested in psychosomatic medicine. While you are travelling abroad, a farmer from an overpopulated, Third-World country comes to consult you about his wife. He tells you that though they have been married several years, they still have no children. He explains to you that in his part of the world a farmer has to have at least three children to survive. He needs two boys to work the farm with him and a third child to go into town, sell the produce, buy supplies, and earn cash.

This farmer dreams that his private interests and the god-spirit of his community are in conflict. He tells you that his community is suffering because they have so little food. It seems as if the anthropos of his community is so over-populated that if the private interests and needs of each of its individual parts were fulfilled, the anthropos would soon be extinguished. The god of the community in the farmer's dream is disturbing his personal goals by preventing the fertility of his wife. This 'disturbance' is not necessarily directed against him, for it benefits the entire community and, indirectly, him as well. If every part's goals were met, the community would be ruined, and no one would be alive to enjoy the results. Hence, the universal dreambody disturbs the individual and family system of a farmer, threatens his identification as a father, and presses him through his dream and his wife's infertility to see himself as part of the world he lives in. Now he is no longer a farmer from a little village but a member of our world.

THE EMPIRICAL ASPECT OF RELIGIOUS PHILOSOPHY

This example is interesting because the moral of the story sounds something like conventional religious philosophy: Live for others and love your neighbor. The difference between this perennial philosophy and our example is that religious ideas have been, until recently, like dreams which have not had to become true. The experience of being members of a larger body is becoming an unavoidable necessity upon which the future of our planet obviously depends. Perhaps this experience will become more available to everyone if we consider that we not only influence the world we live in, but like our farmer, we too are strongly touched by the overall situation of the earth.

CHANGES IN PERSONAL ATTITUDE

Until now, we have been overjoyed with improving our ability at understanding details. We developed the lens, then the microscope, and finally the electron microscope. We hoped that increased ability at understanding little details would mean finally understanding the mechanical behavior of our universe. However, there seems to be no minute mechanical detail which is final. Looking at detail does not explain why we can be in several places at once or why synchronicities occur in which we suddenly connect to other cities beyond our range of communication.

The concept of the global dreambody and its corollaries, the holomovement of David Bohm, Jung's collective unconscious, the anthropos myths of various cultures, and modern quantum theory, imply that working on ourselves is an even more serious business than we previously realized. Changing ourselves, even a little bit, theoretically changes the whole world. This is what the Taoists have always claimed. When we work on ourselves, on a client's individual problem, or a family difficulty, we are doing, in our own individual way, world politics. Inversely, the personal body problems and relationship difficulties we have are, like those of our farmer, influenced, perhaps even organized, by the development of the larger anthropos in which we live. This anthropos then is not really outside of us; it is part of our psychology. The world is a channel for us, a dream figure, a part of our personal story, an expression of ourselves. As long as we experience the world only as a disturber of our fate, we will never have that feeling for the world which is necessary to save it through changing ourselves.

The next great step in our individuation process, therefore, is to discover, feel, see, hear, and relate to the world as if it were a part of us, realizing that we too are a part of its development. To be a person in the latter half of the twentieth century means realizing that we have a personal *and* planetary development. These two aspects of personal development go together; the planetary goals of humankind relativize our egotism, and the ego's goals give the fiery spirit of the world, in all of us, a root in the earth.

INDIVIDUATION AND THE GLOBAL DREAMBODY

In India, experiencing oneself as the Atman or the anthropos has long been the goal for all human beings. For us, this would mean that each of us experiences the conflicts and problems which we read about in the newspaper in ourselves. Imagine what the world would be like if people would read the newspapers as if they were reading about themselves. When they read about a lethal gas leak poisoning thousands of people, they would also be concerned about their own smoking habit. When they get upset with a dictator for unjustly imprisoning people, they would find out how they do that to themselves and others, as well as considering how to deal with the actual dictator.

LOCAL AND GLOBAL INTERVENTIONS

In working with the body problems of an individual we need two points of view, a local and a global one. For example, if someone has a bad case of dandruff, his body awareness will be increased. He will try to find local solutions to the dandruff problem, he will buy new shampoos, massage his scalp, and wash his hair more thoroughly.

Most psychosomatic problems do not disappear with only

local treatment because they require global treatment as well. In dreambody work, the process worker has to tell the client to continue using his local treatments but also to learn how to find a more global solution for his itchy scalp. How does he experience it? If the proprioceptive experience of itchiness leads to punching and other aggressive expressions, then the global treatment for the individual will include changing a passive attitude into a more aggressive one. The local treatment will remain a change in shampoos!

GLOBAL DREAMBODY WORK WITH THE WORLD

How does the theory of local and global interventions apply to our present, very practical world situations? How can we apply it to problems like overpopulation, extreme poverty, illness, energy shortages, and environmental abuses? These questions are obviously too large to be dealt with in detail here, yet for the sake of completion they must be mentioned.

Local dreambody work for the planet includes attempts to inhibit overpopulation, to distribute food and wealth more evenly, to increase medical research, and to raise collective awareness of atomic power, oil, and other energy resources. Global intervention, however, requires processing the psychology of the entire planet.

Global dreambody work requires each of us, as individuals, to be our complete selves in any given moment, for our behavior touches the entire community around us. A single individual who brings up his double signals can change an entire city. This is demonstrated in an example I recently came across during one of my jobs for a large city.

CITY CHANGES

Among the tasks the city hired me for was working with the widespread heroin addiction that this city suffered from. The discussion among the city officials was at a standstill because the members had become hopeless. Apparently everyone had tried repeatedly to deal with the problems at hand, but had failed because of the complexity of the project.

Moreover, the ill-temperedness of one member of the city team soured the entire atmosphere. He sat in his corner, growling misanthropically at the proceedings. Seeing that the meeting wasn't going anywhere, I encouraged him to bring out his (secondary) growls. Naturally, he insisted they were not present. With a little encouragement, however, he not only entered into a rage against me, but against all psychologists in the world. 'How,' he said, 'can you people claim to be of any help when you are unaware of the real problems facing the city? You psychologists are just dumb!'

His attack hurt me and caused me to lose my ability to retain an overview of the situation. My pride was injured and I could not concede that there was an element of truth in what he said: he knew a lot more about city politics than I! Luckily one of my co-workers behaved as if she were badly hurt by his attack. By doing so she picked up the injured part and relieved me of my hurt feelings long enough to realize that this man's secondary process had changed. Before he was simply angry; now he was secondarily asking to be the group leader! I encouraged him to do so. 'Stop being so timid,' I said to him, 'and lead us, tell us what to do. Take over!' He immediately said that what we really needed to do was to learn more about heroin and why it did what it did to addicts and to the city. 'Facts,' he courageously and belligerently called for, 'not feelings!'

Thus, I began to tell the group about some of my experiences with long-time heroin addicts. I explained how drug problems were dealt with in different cultures, especially in China by Chairman Mao. Everyone was fascinated by the topic and the original hopelessness was transformed into a lively and spirited discussion about why certain methods cannot work in a democratic country. The session ended with practical recommendations for understanding the heroin problem as a symptom of the city's need to change.

When processed, this man's bad temper turned out to be the transforming element in an otherwise hopeless meeting. Working with the negativity of one and bringing it out in a large group lead to a change of attitude in the entire city.

The usual local solutions to heroin addiction, drug education and medical and therapeutical approaches were amplified in this case by a global city-wide change in awareness. And this awareness was stimulated by processing the ill temper of a frustrated member of a government meeting.

WORLD WAR?

This example shows how working with individuals in an immediate field can produce global effects in a city. But will the same process be effective in dealing with something as acute and as serious as a world war? In principle it should, but practically I think not, because the world is a much larger place than a city. The effects of single individuals upon the environment take much longer to create global solutions in a world than in a city. It will take a good many individuals who are aware of their relationship processes to help instigate global changes.

Today, when two nations anywhere enter into a conflict, we all find ourselves on the verge of a third world war. Naturally, local solutions and immediate conflict resolutions will be more important than ever before. Somebody is going to have to get to the conflicting part of the anthropos, to its local inflammation, disarm the fighters, and keep them from using their nuclear weapons. But God help us if we rely only upon local problem solvers, the United Nations, or local politics to keep the minor inflammation from developing into a raging world fever.

Since we are all pressed to be members of this planet, we are all politicians whether we like it or not. Therefore, we are all responsible for processing global conflicts in order to turn the threat of a disastrous world war into greater understanding and relationship. Certainly we will have to improve our local treatments of world war, but we shall also need to create global planetary therapy.

FACTORS IN GLOBAL THERAPY

The immense anthropos we live in must learn to process its conflicts. This means that many of us are going to have to develop the courage to enter the conflicts we have with our relatives, the letter carriers, butchers, and policemen, and process them.

However, courage alone will never be sufficient because it leads only to winning and losing, and, as we know by now, no one wins a relationship battle without injuring the relationship. We need more than courage. A global treatment for war will require each of us to enter into a new kind of war, a battle which is fought not only to win but also for the sake of discovering oneself and one's opponent. I am thinking of war without bloodshed, an interaction between parties who are aware that the existence of each is necessary for the life of the whole. Each party must have a basic awareness of the opponent as a necessary part of life and of their conflict as an unavoidable process requiring awe and respect.

Courage, awareness, awe, and respect are necessary but still insufficient to process these global conflicts. Precise knowledge about behavior in relationships is needed. When it comes to knowledge, however, we are only in the beginning of our studies. At least we know how important it is to notice double signals and employ gentle methods for translating their often mysterious signs into mundane terms. Remember that many wars come about through misunderstandings and misinterpretations of signals. Learning to be clear about our own and other's signals will turn a lot of conflicts into rich relationships.

TRAGIC AND SERIOUS RIFTS

But even correct interpretation of signals could sometimes be insufficient, especially in those situations where either you or your opponent are blind and deaf to the other's behavior. Making a program out of clear and correct communication will never be a panacea for conflict because it is frequently important for one of the partners to remain unconscious and not notice what the other is really doing (see pages 51 and 52). Remember, unconsciousness is also a process and has a function; it protects the individual from opening up to the empirical reality of the world around him and allows him to remain internal and process unconscious beliefs and myths.

This is frequently the reality with opponents who insist that the other is the aggressor. What are the options when someone continues to accuse you of terrible aggression, even if you deny it or accept it as partly true?

If you admit to aggression, then you can work constructively upon your disagreements. If you are not feeling aggressive, however, you will soon be dreamed up, become angry, and find yourself in a battle and acting aggressively. Now your oponent is justified in his accusations. If this type of interaction occurs several times, it will lead to a tragic rift in relationships. On a planetary level, it could lead to world war.

THE FUNCTION OF UNCONSCIOUSNESS

In such serious cases, what choices do we have in dealing with this difficult personal and collective behavior? If, after you carefully check out your signals, your opponent still does not believe you, you will have to consider the possibility that he is projecting. But be careful! Telling someone that he is projecting or dreaming you up is usually not very useful because these fancy terms are really meant to criticize and avoid the reality of the opponent.

Remember that there might be an important function to your opponent's prevailing unconsciousness. One of its functions is that you yourself will have to believe in your own feelings and not in your opponent's projections. But now it's important that you examine your motives. Are you only interested in winning? If not, you might consider the possibility of supporting your opponent's projections! It will be essential that you allow yourself to be consciously dreamed up so as to help your opponent complete the process of unconsciousness he is caught in. This means nothing less than consciously acting like the aggressive figure of his projection while simultaneously preserving your external overview of the entire process for the benefit of all.

For the party caught in the midst of unconsciousness, I have only one recommendation: don't believe in your partner, not yet at least. Believe in your experiences and your perceptions. Though they may create a lot of pain for you and the world, they are a core conflict which has been searching for light since the beginning of civilization. Processed with respect, this conflict and its unconsciousness will not only teach you about unknown parts of yourself, but will also force the world around you to enlightenment about relationships and conflicts in general. For without such enlightenment, you will continue to search for war and aggression in those around you.

When enough of us learn about this experience, we shall find ourselves in the beginning of a global treatment for world war. Such awareness is a world project; our evolution as a planet will depend upon such a form of global development in our awareness. Mere political changes, including local and temporary solutions to acute world conflicts, only postpone the crises. These superficial changes are never as far-reaching as global changes in which the entire human environment changes. Temporary and local solutions only force the conflict underground, and thus it breaks out anew in unpredictable ways.

The question remains, will the kind of process-oriented awareness recommended by this text be possible for enough individuals to create a global solution to world war? Only the future evolution of our planet will be able to answer this question. I personally suspect that the answer will be 'yes' since we have no other choice. We can no longer pretend that we are solely loving and peaceful beings. Nor can we continue to believe that it's possible to grow more powerful in our defenses without destroying our planet.

THE SPIRITUAL WARRIOR

Thus, we shall each have to start upon the path of self-knowledge and reach a stage of completion we have only dreamed about until now, a stage of highly developed awareness. The kind of individual and group awareness I am pointing to has a spiritual quality about it; it is neither a peace movement – which is based upon negating the process of conflict – nor an ordinary warlike movement – which is driven by banal hatred, but it is a spiritual warrior's zealous path of serving the fiery global spirit that our lives create.

Chapter 13
THINKING IT OVER

Since this book is concerned primarily with relationships, the natural conclusion would be to ask the reader for his comments, questions, and observations. The following questions and comments are an approximation, I hope, of what the reader would like to ask. I suspect that there are no complete answers. Nevertheless, this last chapter summarizes certain aspects and difficult points of the book and leads into areas of psychology where there are no clear answers and where further research is required. Readers with questions not presented here should write to me directly. I will include their questions in future editions of this work.

Question: I have finished reading the book, and I must admit that I am still afraid of relationship conflicts. I fear stored-up emotion and am scared to approach such affect directly. Can relationship conflicts be dangerous?
Answer: Relationship conflicts which have been neglected and which have been building up for many years can be very dramatic. I never recommend working on relationships unless people feel they must. If one member of a couple refuses to come, I support this too. Frequently, the great edges dividing people arise because someone fears that getting close to emotions will drive him crazy. A family therapist not trained in process work may possibly push people over their edges before they are ready. A process worker, however, does not stress emotions, confrontation,

openness, detachment, or any program. A process worker with an adequate training follows the way of nature. Thus, when people withdraw or back away out of fear, he supports their introversion and need for safety. When they move toward each other, he encourages confrontation. When one steps out and asks for individual help and support, he supports this as well. In this way, dangerous situations, even with psychotic people, can be transformed into useful processes.

On the other hand, I advise people to risk the dangers and fears when a chronic body problem, terminal disease, or periodic breakdown is present. These circumstances favor the emotional risk since process work frequently clarifies and reduces psychotic imbalance and chronic disease.

I remember one seminar in which a woman suffering from asthma worked on her hurt feelings with a man in the seminar. She waited a long time, then finally got over her edge against her emotions and pleaded with the man for more attention in their relationship. He refused and then provoked her by mimicking her. Her asthma immediately came back in an attack which then subsided when she said that her needs were real, and if they weren't accepted, she could almost die. She saw the significance of her chronic body symptom. She herself was constantly making fun of herself for having needs instead of appreciating them. She was killing herself by feeling guilty for her needs and feelings.

Question: Relationship problems are difficult for therapists, too. It's almost impossible to sit in the middle of a couple's tension and listen to the conflicts and accusations and see all that pain.

Answer: Relationship work is not for every therapist. Nevertheless, it is good for a therapist to know about such work and useful to realize that he, too, has certain blocks and edges. In fact, it is very important for a therapist to encounter his weak spots, his blocks, and his edges. Otherwise, he may inadvertently inhibit a patient from clearing up relationship problems, chronic body problems, and psychotic corners because of his own limitations. Frequently, a therapist covers up his fear of emotions and conflict with weak theories and futile discussions.

Question: I have a bottom-line belief that process work with relationships may break longstanding, cultural rules favoring harmony, peace, and happiness. Is there not some way of solving conflict *and* avoiding pain?

Answer: There is no doubt that processing secondary phenomena brings you over cultural edges. As I have said, I do not encourage people to break cultural patterns unless they are forced to do so. I tend to support primary cultural processes. Though certain rules should be broken, they should be done consciously and with great awareness.

I, too, dislike emotional turmoil. The only thing I can say in favor of risking the pain and turmoil involved is that if you compare the pain and turmoil involved in slow, terminal diseases such as cancer and multiple sclerosis, then two or three hours of relationship work seems to be nothing less than heaven on earth. In a way, a really sick person is lucky to have a big relationship problem because his partner can often be more potent medicine than any pill or therapist.

Question: What are some of the statements most often found on the other side of the edge?

Answer: The most common repressed emotions and statements that surface when one crosses an edge are: 'If you don't love me, then I'll die.' 'You'll have to kill me before I'll admit that I feel weak.' 'I want to kill you.' 'I need you.' 'I cannot live without the support of a group.' 'I don't want to need anyone, but I do.' 'I promised myself never to hurt anyone, but I hate people secretly.' 'At heart, I am still a child.' 'I hate family life.'

Question: I am an ordinary person, not an analyst, and I would like to know how I can work on relationship problems alone.

Answer: Anyone can discover their edges which disturb relationships. Just ask yourself, what can you not do in the neighborhood of a certain person, your enemy, your partner? Let's say that you cannot cry or cannot be negative. You need to practice these things. Learning to do process work with yourself or others is a matter of exercise and training. You can practice showing emotions and you can train yourself to be negative in little ways.

The next step in working with yourself is awareness and to do this is also a matter of training. It takes a long time before you realize that the only rules governing relationships are in your own body, your own intuitions, your own dreams. No one can be a better or more trustworthy guru for you than your own process. Thus, if you want to function as an independent person on this earth, ask your own body, look at your own double signals for information about being with others. But be careful: If you are characteristically strong, you will miss your signals of weakness. If you identify with being weak, you will not notice when your fists are clenched.

The last step in process work is a matter of fate. It is becoming a warrior. If you lack the courage to have conflict, you should consider relationship a matter of growth and knowledge. Your awareness is going to change you and help your partner to grow and change as well. Conflict is the beginning of self-knowledge. Relationships will cost you your precious identity but may also bring you a larger picture of your real personality. So wait until your energy and courage come together, then go to knowledge as a warrior goes to war.

After you have worked on your own edges, your awareness, and your courage, you are ready to turn towards your partner. Help him to do the same, ask him about his edges with you, listen to them, and then watch the communication signals arise between you.

Question: Is it possible to work on relationship problems when one of the partners is absent?
Answer: Certainly. My empirical observations indicate that the same problems which come up with a loved one occur with others as well. In case the partner of your client is not

willing to come to therapy, keep in mind that any problem you yourself have with the client may mirror the ones he is having with his partner. If you are lucky enough to get into a relationship conflict with your client, you may be able to help him with all of his relationships. Relationships often seem to be processes looking for people to populate them.

I remember a startling example in one of my seminars. A woman worked on a problem she had with a man who was not in the seminar and who had refused, over the years, to see her. She chose one of the men in the seminar to act out the conflict with her. But she became so violent that he got frightened and asked her to stop fighting and talk. Her kinesthetic behavior did not work with him because there was too much aggression, and also because the role playing was only an act, not the real thing. To be more realistic, she chose another man in the seminar with whom she had a real, though minor, conflict. There, too, she became very kinesthetic, emotional, and aggressive. She quickly brought her partner to an edge. He was visually and verbally oriented, and she liked acting everything out. She literally pushed him so far that he finally physically forced her to stop moving and start talking. This, of course, was just her edge, what she needed to learn. Her emotionality forced him to break down his cool and express more feeling than he was accustomed to.

The important point here is that the process around this woman was independent of the people she had problems with. Though the issues were different in all cases, the process of having to talk about difficulties was the same.

Question: In a previous question, you mentioned that a relationship can be worked on with an absent partner through a conflict with the therapist. How can you tell when the client is in a relationship channel with you?
Answer: When the client talks constantly of an absent party, you know he is in a relationship channel. When he dreams about conversations between dream figures, you can be sure he is going to get into conflicts with you and others to learn more about these interactions. When he falls in love

with you, hates you, criticizes you, doubts you, or brings up third parties who have talked about you, these are all times when he is having an unconscious conflict with you. When you yourself can no longer concentrate, when you have strong feelings which chip away at your persona, when you defend yourself, deny accusations, or begin to dream about your client, then it is an accurate guess to say that you both are in a relationship channel.

When the therapist is in a relationship channel too, he can no longer act only as the therapist. Now he must relinquish his control over the situation, his primary process, or his programs of therapy. It means that he is now a part of the field and that he is going to lose some of his awareness. He swims or drowns, depending upon how much knowledge he has of his own double signals, how much strength and courage he has to admit to the client's accusations, and how much insight he has into his own dreams.

The therapist needs to know that when he is in a relationship channel he will come across his edges, and his own ability to get over them is going to encourage his client to do the same. One of the reasons some therapists never encourage their clients to develop too quickly is that a client's development pushes the therapist over an edge. No therapist likes his own edges, and hence, if he is not careful, he can hinder the client's development by keeping him safely underdeveloped in order that he maintain the status quo.

As long as the therapist and the client get along together, their relationship channel is not strongly occupied and other issues come to the fore. The worst troubles begin when the therapist gets negative feedback from the client or when the therapist begins to dislike the client. The latter feels this and complains. At this point, the therapist frequently defends himself by claiming that the client is neurotic or is projecting some early, negative parental image. The therapist calls upon the magic spells of the therapeutic setting to make the client feel guilty and to bind him to therapy. Alternatively, the therapist, squirming around his own edge, may recommend that the client leave therapy and reenter the world to work out his relationship conflicts there.

If the therapist is lucky, the client will stay with him long enough until awareness and change is constellated, and the insidious hopelessness of unworked-out relationships transforms into hopeful and warm friendship.

Question: How does the spirit of the universal dreambody influence personal relationships today?

The answer to this question is too vast for me. At best I can only say that our planetary problems strongly influence our personal lives. One of the most characteristic aspects of the universal dreambody today is collective interest in, and fear of, world war. This fascination touches the core of all our relationships.

Because of the increased world tension, it seems that there will be more and more individuals who will be willing to bear and process relationship tension. The fear of nuclear war is part of the same pattern as the courage to go over what were previously considered impossible edges in personal life. The increasing interest and ability to process conflicts reveals great depth to the stream of relationship which connects us all, depths which appeared earlier only as religious beliefs which were usually inaccessible to daily life. This new ability to process anger and jealousy increases our hopes for a better world and will eventually contribute to defusing world tension. Working on relationships with yourself, your partner, the police, city officials, teachers, friends and local politicians will, if nothing else, reduce the interest in annihilating foreign countries.

One of the paradoxes of relationship processes which I have stressed in this work is that the 'lowest' drives of human existence, namely, jealousy, competitiveness and anger become the door to something we could call infinite or divine love, once the conflict which they create has been processed. We are always fearful of entering into conflict, and it is truly shocking when this love and deep connection with other people emerges from the neglected, secret recesses of confirmed hopelessness.

BIBLIOGRAPHY

Bateson, Gregory, *Steps to an Ecology of Mind*, Ballantine Books, New York, 1972.

Birdswhistell, Ray, *Kinesics and Context, Essays on Body Motion Communication*, University of Pennsylvania Press, Philadelphia, 1970.

Capra, Fritz, *The Tao of Physics*, Wildwood House, London, 1975.

Capra, Fritz, *The Turning Point; Science, Society and the Rising Culture*, Wildwood House, London, 1982.

Chomsky, Noam, *Language and Mind*, Harcourt Brace Jovanovich, New York, 1968.

von Franz, M.L., *Patterns of Creativity Mirrored in Creation Myths*, Spring, Dallas, 1978.

von Franz, M.L., *Mirrors of the Soul, Projection and Inner Centering*, Northwestern, Evanston, Ill. 1980.

von Franz, M.L., 'The Inferior Function,' in *Jung's Typology*, together with J. Hillman, Spring, Dallas.

Gunter, 'Die Koepernikanische Revolution in der Psychotherapie: Familiendynamik' (Zeitschrift), 1980.

Gunter, *Social Change, Stress and Mental Health in the Pearl of the Alps*, Springer, New York, 1979.

Haley, J., *Problem Solving Therapy*, Jossey-Bass, San Francisco, 1976.

Jung, C.G., *Complete Works* vols, 2, 15, 16., Routledge & Kegan Paul, London, 1982; Princeton, New Jersey.

Kohut, H., *The Restoration of the Self*, International Universities Press, New York, 1977.

Kohut, H., 'The Two Analyses of Mr. Z.' *International Journal of Psychoanalysis*, vol. 6., Paris, 1979, p.3.

Mandances, Cloe, *Strategic Family Therapy*, Jossey-Bass, London, 1981.

Miller, Alice, *The Drama of the Gifted Child and the Search for the True Self*, trans. by Ruth Ward, Faber, London, 1983.

Minuchin, Salvadore, *Families and Family Therapy*, Harvard University Press, Cambridge, Mass., 1974.

Minuchin, Salvadore, *Psychosomatic Families: Anorexia Nervosa in Context*, Harvard University Press, Cambridge, 1978.

Mindell, Arnold, *Dreambody*, Sigo Press, Boston, 1982.

Mindell, Arnold, *Working with the Dreaming Body*, Routledge & Kegan Paul, London and Boston, 1985.

Mindell, Arnold, *River's Way*, Routledge & Kegan Paul, London and Boston, 1985.

Schwartz, Nathan, 'Archetypal Factors and Underlying Sexual Acting Out in the Transference-countertransference Process,' *Chiron*, Spring, 1984.

Wilbur, Ken, ed., *The Holographic Paradigm and Other Paradoxes*, Shambhala, Boulder, 1982.

INDEX

PENGUIN

ARKANA

NEW AGE BOOKS FOR MIND, BODY & SPIRIT

A SELECTION OF TITLES

Herbal Medicine for Everyone Michael McIntyre

'The doctor treats but nature heals.' With an increasing consciousness of ecology and a move towards holistic treatment, the value of herbal medicine is now being fully recognized. Discussing the history and principles of herbal medicine and its application to a wide range of diseases and ailments, this illuminating book will prove a source of great wisdom.

The Tarot Alfred Douglas

The puzzle of the original meaning and purpose of the Tarot has never been fully resolved. An expert in occult symbolism, Alfred Douglas explores the traditions, myths and religions associated with the cards, investigates their historical, mystical and psychological importance and shows how to use them for divination.

Views from the Real World G. I. Gurdjieff

Only through self-observation and self-exploration, Gurdjieff asserted, could man develop his consciousness. To this end he evolved exercises through which awareness could be heightened and enlightenment attained. *Views from the Real World* contains his talks and lectures on this theme as he travelled from city to city with his pupils. What emerges is his immensely human approach to self-improvement.

Riding the Horse Backwards Arnold and Amy Mindell

Arnold Mindell is the originator of perhaps the most inspiring 'school' of healing we have in the West now, process work, and in this running narrative of one of his workshops, which he gave with Amy Mindell at the Esalen community in the United States, we're taken to the heart of the magic.

PENGUIN

ARKANA

NEW AGE BOOKS FOR MIND, BODY & SPIRIT

A SELECTION OF TITLES

Working on Yourself Alone: Inner Dreambody Work
Arnold Mindell

Western psychotherapy and Eastern meditation are two contrasting ways of learning more about one's self. The first depends heavily on the powers of the therapist. *Process-oriented* meditation, however, can be used by the individual as a means of resolving conflicts and increasing awareness from within. Using meditation, dream work and yoga, this remarkable book offers techniques that you can develop on your own, allowing the growth of an individual method.

Neo-Astrology   Michel Gauquelin

Michel Gauquelin's Neo-Astrology is a frugal science that discards much of the traditional horoscope, and suggests that five planets only – Saturn, Jupiter, Mars, Venus and the Moon – affect us. This important work shows that the French psychologist and statistician may be pointing towards nothing less than a new model of the universe.

Homage to the Sun: The Wisdom of the Magus of Strovolos
Kyriacos C. Markides

Homage to the Sun continues the adventure into the mysterious and extraordinary world of the spiritual teacher and healer Daskalos, the 'Magus of Strovolos'. The logical foundations of Daskalos' world of other dimensions are revealed to us – invisible masters, past-life memories and guardian angels, all explained by the Magus with great lucidity and scientific precision.

The Eagle's Gift   Carlos Castaneda

In the sixth book in his astounding journey into sorcery, Castaneda returns to Mexico. Entering once more a world of unknown terrors, hallucinatory visions and dazzling insights, he discovers that he is to replace the Yaqui Indian don Juan as leader of the apprentice sorcerers – and learns of the significance of the Eagle.